"Loyalty" issue/p. 106

DAUGHTERS

On Family and Fatherhood

Also by Gerald Early

DAUGHTERS
On Family and Fatherhood

Gerald Early

Addison-Wesley Publishing Company

Reading, Massachusetts   Menlo Park, California
New York   Don Mills, Ontario
Wokingham, England   Amsterdam   Bonn
Sydney   Singapore   Tokyo   Madrid   San Juan
Paris   Seoul   Milan   Mexico City   Taipei

The author would like to thank Rosalind Early for permission to quote from her diary.

"Dumbo's Ears or How We Begin" has previously appeared in *Northwest Review.*

Library of Congress Cataloging-in-Publication Data
Early, Gerald Lyn.
    Daughters : on family and fatherhood / by Gerald Early.
      p. cm.
    ISBN 0-201-62724-8
    1. Early, Gerald Lyn—Family. 2. Early family. 3. Afro-Americans—Biography. 4. Afro-American children. I. Title.
E185.97.E26A3 1994
973'.0496073'00922—dc20
[B]
                                   94-3006
                                   CIP

Jacket design by Jean Seal
Text design by Greta D. Sibley
Set in 11-pt. Sabon by Greta D. Sibley

1 2 3 4 5 6 7 8 9 10-HD-9897969594
First printing, May 1994

To the Memory of My Father,
Henry Early, Jr., a man I did not know
but the thought of whom
makes me tremble in wonder
at what he knew of his own days

For I prophesy that they will call the days by better names.

—Christopher Smart, *Rejoice in the Lamb*

What thing, in honor, had my father lost,
That need to be revived and breathed in me?

—Shakespeare, *Henry IV, Part II*

For all the saints who from their labors rest,
Who thee by faith before the world confessed,
Thy name, O Jesus, be forever blest.
Alleluia! Alleluia!

—19th-century Christian Hymn

❖ CONTENTS ❖

Sisterhood (handwritten annotation)

To be black & middle class ≫ (handwritten annotation)

*That hundred
of buy the
respect*

DAUGHTERS
On Family and Fatherhood

A STORY OF REARING CHILDREN IN MIDDLE-CLASS AMERICA

For This the foolish father overcareful fathers
Have broke their sleep with thoughts, their brains
with care,
Their bones with industry

   —Shakespeare, *Henry IV, Part II*

In the beginning all about the person.

   —Rosalind Early's diary, frontispiece

This is not a book that I wanted to write, nor that I intended to write. But, clearly, in considering how I arrived at this pass, it is a book that I was destined to write. I do not see it as a kind of extension of the essays that I wrote that featured my daughters. Two in particular, entitled generically "Life with Daughters," were not even directly about my daughters—that is, not exactly. I had in mind certain ideas about women I wanted to explore, to investigate, and using my children to illustrate certain points, to provide a narrative thread, was simply expedient. They actually provided me with a way of talking about women and girlhood while being able, utterly, to avoid the turbulent waters of feminism and womanism and all the other ideological stances that surround the subject these days. That is to say, they gave me an automatic and, I might add, fairly unassailable authority because they were, alas, my daughters, with all the intimacy and intricacy that that relationship entails. To my children, I am immensely grateful for being given the freedom to write about something that interested me and remain true to myself. Surely, others who may have read the "Life with Daughters" essays may think too that I was destined to write this book, but those essays did not lead to this project as a kind of natural creative off-shoot. In fact, I had abandoned the "Life with Daughters" series after only two essays when I had, for a time, thought it might be something grander: a series of a dozen essays taking my daughters to adulthood. I stopped the series not because I did not want to write about them anymore, whether directly or indirectly, but rather because I thought I might leave them to their lives and their privacy. I returned to it—that is, to the idea of writing about them—only because when I asked their permission to do this book, they eagerly granted it.

"Yes," said Rosalind, "we want to tell our story. And we will make sure that you get it right."

"Hey," I said, smiling, "whose book is this, anyway? I'm doing the writing and it is about a *father* and his daughters, just in case you guys forgot."

"We're just going to make sure that you tell the right stories about us, not those ones that you and Mommy are always bringing up," Rosalind said. "After all, you wouldn't have a book if it wasn't for us. Who wants to hear about the life of Gerald Early without daughters?

"And you have to say good things about Mommy," Rosalind continued.

"It shall be done," I replied.

"And you can't get divorced for at least a year after the book comes out, otherwise it will look bad," Rosalind went on.

"I shall try my best to stave off that dreadful possibility," I said, cheekily. "After all, your mother and I have been able to make it through sixteen years of marriage and survive the both of you. We should be able to survive a *book* about the two of you."

"Very funny, Daddy," Rosalind said. "Who writes your material? Do you or can we blame your students?

"Oh yeah," she added. "Make it simple, so a lot of people can read it. None of that *Tuxedo Junction* stuff. I couldn't even read the first page of that book."

"That book was not written for children, you know."

"And it wasn't written for anybody else either. None of that intellectual stuff, Daddy. You've got to get with the program. We gotta sell books here."

"It shall be simple. It shall be short. And it shall give pleasure," I said, paraphrasing Wallace Stevens.

Linnet, who had been unusually quiet through all of this, simply looked up at this point and said, "Yes, this will be *our* book, a book the Early family made."

So, a few days later, each gave me her diary, an utter shock as they scarcely permitted either my wife or me to touch them. The project was launched. And I charged myself with the task of telling a story in which I was central but in which I was absent as well, for my daughters are an existence that is contingent upon me yet fully and freely unimagined by me.

That this is, in part, the story of a middle-class black family or, more precisely put, about middle-class black children is, doubtless, of some interpretative importance, but whatever is said of Linnet and Rosalind here is not meant in any way to be representative or typical of any kind of black experience or anybody's black experience but their own or our own, as the case may be. I was a bit wary about this enterprise in part because when whites write books, generally speaking, the authors are not burdened with speaking for their groups, unless they announce themselves as wishing to do so. A black father writes a book about being a father and he may find himself in the middle of a morass of social, political, and cultural interpretations, as an expert witness for the prosecution, the defense, or whoever else stakes a claim. I am sure that there are millions of loving black families and loving black fathers in the United States, and this book needn't be seen, nor should it be, as a weighty example of something or providing propaganda—of any sort—for any factionalized aspect of the "race problem," as I might touchingly call it. (My fellow African Americans hardly need me to be so presumptuous as that!)

Alas, the business of class in this book is not so easily solved, resolved, or even addressed. It is, clearly, a worse conundrum than race—a tangled, very freighted affair of associations and entrapments, anxieties and desires, from which one will never be free. Consider this:

Perhaps a year ago, Rosalind, in the failed execution of a school science project, ruined our dining-room table. It was a table that Ida, my wife, had for years coveted and which, in our more flush times, she was finally able to buy. There had been some talk, in the immediate aftermath of the incident, of having Rosalind pay for refinishing the table by giving up her allowance (probably for the rest of her childhood and adolescence, as I recall the expense of the refinishing) and her savings. Rosalind, in her hysterical repentance, indeed volunteered to do this, and Ida, in her anger of the moment, accepted. But a few weeks later, when feelings had calmed, life went back to its normal routine. Rosalind continued to get her allowance, and Ida returned to her the bankbook that, in her fit of guilty despair, Rosalind had handed over as a down payment on repairing the table.

It was not long after this that Rosalind came into my study one day, feeling a bit expansive. "You guys are the greatest parents in the world!" she said generously.

"And what have we done," I asked with equal expansiveness, "to merit this abundant, excessive recognition of our humble talents as care providers."

"Hey, I thought you guys were going to kill me for messing up the dining-room table, but you didn't," Rosalind said.

"Well, what did you think we were going to do," I asked, "hit you? No one has ever hit you. Why would you think we would?"

"How am I supposed to know that, if I do something really bad?" Rosalind asked. "You guys won't hit me unless I do it. And that's a kind of dangerous way of finding out."

"I guess you're right," I agreed. "But I can hardly think of anything we would hit you for. Besides, you're too big for spanking and that kind of stuff."

She started to walk from the room but then stopped. "Say, Daddy, how old were you when your mother last spanked you?"

I thought for a moment. "Ten," I replied simply, realizing as I spoke that that was how old Rosalind was now.

"Wow, you must have done something really bad. I didn't think your mother would spank you."

"Yes," I said, turning back to the computer, "I did something really bad."

Rosalind quietly considered this for a moment. "Well, what did you do?"

I sighed. I felt slightly uneasy. I could remember it very well although I did not, at that moment, wish to dredge it up. (I had never told anyone the story before, in part because I never wanted, in any way, for anyone to question how I had been reared.) But Rosalind, someone whom I was rearing, seemed as good a person as anyone to tell it to now.

"Well?" she pressed.

"I broke an egg."

"Is that all? You got a spanking for breaking an egg?" she asked incredulously.

"It was worse than a spanking," I said, turning around suddenly to face her. "She slapped my face, hard, two or three times. She called me a name. She was furious with me because it was the last egg in the house, you see." I began to stammer, something I almost never do unless I am distraught, unnerved. And as I began to recall the incident I could feel my body growing hot.

"It was the last egg in the house, you know." I began to speak slowly. "And she told me not to mess with it. But I got this odd idea, this very odd idea, that I could cook this egg myself. You know, sometimes you get a notion that you can't shake. But when I tried, I broke the shell, and, you know, it just splattered on the floor. I was, well, sorta shocked. And I tried with a spoon, you know, to scoop it up from the floor. I don't know why I tried that. I guess I thought maybe I could put it back in the shell. Maybe my mother would never know it was broken. And that's how my mother, you know, found me. Just like that, trying to scoop the egg up with a tiny spoon and just, I don't know, just kinda spreading it around. I had sticky egg yolk on my fingers." I could feel myself reliving

every humiliating moment as if it had happened only yesterday.

"She was so angry. She just hit me in the face
before she knew what she was doing. She hit
me and hollered at me. She said, 'You miserable ass!' just like that. I just kinda stumbled
backwards.

"You know," I said, with a wan smile, "it
must have looked crazy, if you could have seen
it. Like two people doing some kind of bad
dancing. It was like we had been stepping on
each other's feet."

My voice was beginning to waver and I
wanted to stop. But Rosalind just stood there,
silently, and actually looking a bit aghast. My
body was burning with shock and mortifica-
tion. I could feel my eyes well with tears. It was
the slow rush of being overwhelmed by what
Theodore Roethke called "the grim digits of
old pain." As I told the story, it was as if it
were happening all over again. Why am I telling this to Rosalind? I thought.

"I was so ashamed, so ashamed." I was trembling now. "I was just so ashamed. Not because
my mother, you know, was mad. She had a
right to be mad. She should have hit me. My
mother was very good to me and, you know, I
should not have tried to cook that egg. I was

so ashamed because I knew, then, at that moment, that I was poor, if one egg meant that much. And I was so ashamed, I mean, that I was poor like that. So damn ashamed of the both of us."

I could not face Rosalind then, because I was on the verge of crying. My whole body was convulsing. I was on the verge of breaking down entirely. So I simply, abruptly, got up and left my study, computer on, Rosalind just standing there, without ending the story, without explanation.

"I will never be middle class," I told Ida once, "no matter how much money I might be fortunate enough to make. I will always be poor. You die in the class you were born into. It's the law of life."

But there is another story about class to be told. Shortly after I signed to write this book, Linnet came to me and asked if we might add another bathroom to our house, the biggest house we have ever lived in, if the book was successful.

"Why do you want another bathroom?" I asked.

"Because I can't stand sharing the bathroom

with Ros. She's a complete slob, a pig. She leaves her dirty clothes all over the floor, never flushes the toilet, leaves big globs of toothpaste in the sink, and never hangs up her towel. I can't stand her and I want my own bathroom."

"Well, when I was a kid..." I began.

"Listen, Daddy, No offense. But I don't want to hear any stories about how twenty people used one bathroom when you were a kid and everybody got along just fine. You're not poor anymore."

Later that evening, Rosalind came to me with, amazingly, the same request.

"I can't stand sharing a bathroom with Linnet. She leaves her rubber bands from her braces all over the sink. She never brushes her teeth. She leaves bloody underwear and sanitary napkins all over the floor. And she's always bossing me around and telling me about how to wear my headbands, how to do this, how to do that. I can't stand her and I want my own bathroom."

"We'll see," I said noncommittally.

Later I exclaimed to Ida, "I can't believe the kids we're rearing. All they think about are creature comforts. They want new bathrooms and such. It's outrageous! They think that if the book makes a lot of money, they should be able to buy things! What about doing something creative with the money or even giving it away? When I grew up, I lived in a house that was barely the size of the living room and dining room we have now."

"You're not poor anymore," Ida said simply. "Besides, if they want a new bathroom from their share of the book's profits, what's so wrong with that? They're children, so they want to do childish things. Would you like them better if they were little Spartans or little Stoics or little Franciscans or something? And if you were their age, would you be thinking about giving away money? Did you have children so that they could repeat your childhood because it was so great? I don't think so. Besides, when was the last time you wanted to do something so grand and noble with money? I figure they could want better things than a bathroom, but they could want worse too. Good night."

But Ida was wrong about giving away money, and I told her this story as she pretended to fall asleep: When I was sixteen, I had three cloth-covered books about karate—Mas Oyama's *What Is Karate?* and *This Is Karate* and M. Nakayama's *Dynamic Karate*—that cost about twenty dollars each, an extraordinary amount of money to pay for a book in 1968. I had worked hard on my paper route and as a clerk in a cheap jewelry store to save up the money for the books. There were two boys in the neighborhood, a few years younger, who loved to come over to my house just to look at those books. I knew how much they coveted them. But they had no money and could not possibly afford to buy them. So one day, out of the blue, I gave each of them—they were brothers—a book. To one I gave *Dynamic Karate* and to the other *What Is Karate?* and I kept *This Is Karate* (which I have to this day) for myself.

"Why would you want to give away those expensive books that you worked so hard to get to those ragamuffin boys?" my mother asked querulously. "That doesn't make any sense. Let them go out and work for them just like you did."

"But, Ma," I said, "they really wanted the books. The books meant more to them than to me. They walked over here all the time to read them."

"Those boys just gonna mess those books up," my mother said. "You just wasting your money giving them books."

"Maybe they will," I said, a little disappointed because I felt that she was probably right. The books were important to me, the first hardcover books I had ever bought and the beginning of what I thought would be a huge martial-arts library. I felt, for a moment, a certain regret over giving the books away. But I convinced myself that on the whole it was a good thing to do, "a kind of socialism for the poor," I said to Ida.

I sat on the edge of the bed and I heard Ida's breathing. I thought she had drifted away to sleep. After a moment, I heard an explosively loud guffaw.

"What a story!" she said, rolling across the bed, laughing. "What a story! Get out the violins! 'Socialism for the poor,' my eye! First, you probably gave them those books because those boys were getting on your nerves coming over there bothering you about seeing them. You thought that the best way to get rid of them would be just to give them the books."

"That's not true," I said, petulantly. "Those boys were like brothers to me."

"Yeah," Ida said, skeptically, "sure they were. Why don't you just admit that you gave them the books because you thought that you could probably make enough money in the future to buy the books again if you wanted them? And you probably would have too, except you lost interest in all that kung fu nonsense, so that was that."

"Okay," I said, thoroughly annoyed. "Just denigrate me, just dismiss my childhood."

"Nobody's dismissing your childhood," Ida rejoined, chuckling. "But you've got to admit, you're just like your mother: you don't believe in benevolent charity, especially for the poor, because you grew up with the attitude of all poor people: the world is a 'get-over' place. So, don't give anybody anything unless you want to be played for a sucker. That's your mother and it's you too. All giving away those books showed was that you, like a lot of middle-class people, believe in convenient charity. You got rid of those boys, plus won their admiration and gained some authority over them. Class is a state of mind. It's got nothing to do with the money in your pocket. Try those little ghetto tales of solidarity on your white readers. Don't try them on me. Remember I grew up around working-class black folk too. Good night."

As she rolled over to her side, I couldn't, for the life of me, figure out how I lost that battle of wits.

Ida, then, scored one last blow: "Besides," she said from beneath the covers, "you told me the story before but with a much more honest spin, about how it was proof that you were going to get out of the ghetto but the boys you gave the books to were not. You're just as confused about your class orientation as everybody else in America."

"Well, if I'm not poor anymore, I'm not rich either. And I'm not interested in building bathrooms," I said lamely.

"Good night," Ida said.

To be black and middle-class is to live in a sort of make-believe world but a different world than E. Franklin Frazier suggests: constantly in dread of what you are and whimsically fabricating what you were. It is like being, as Linnet once brilliantly and accidentally said about herself, "a discontinuous person."

I might add here simply that this book is suffused with a kind of Christian thought (but nothing for which I would use such an elevated term as *theology*). Let us say that this book has a certain subtle preoccupation with, to use a quaint word, righteousness, and, to use a more quaint word, mercy. And it would seem that a family is as good a place to be concerned about these matters as, say, society at large or this incredibly unjust world as we know it. This, I suppose, is hardly surprising for a man whose personal hero is Edmund Campion—whom my daughters call Champion and whom my wife thought for a goodly time was the hero of mystery novels. My children are not, in fact, Christians, in the sense that they have never been baptized, although they do attend a church on a fairly regular basis. In other words, I like to think of this book, in part, as a story of family and its faith struggle. I suppose that I am deeply devoted to my religion, to the faith—that is, if I might ever learn to be worthy of it.

I remember as a boy hearing the Bells of Joy sing a song played on the black gospel radio station nearly every Sunday called "Let's Talk About Jesus" and other groups such as the Harmonizing Four singing "All Things Are Possible (If You Only Believe)," the Dixie Hummingbirds' "In The Morning (When The Dark Clouds Roll Away)," the Davis Sisters, the Caravans, Mahalia Jackson's "How I Got Over," a favorite of my mother, and the Golden Gate Gospel Quartet singing a song I learned in Sunday School:

> Children, Go Where I Send Thee,
> O, How Shall I Send Thee?

Well, I'm gonna send you
Five by Five
Five for the five that came back alive
Four for the four that stood at the door
And Three for the Hebrew children
And Two for Paul and Silas
And One for the little, bitty baby
Born, Born, Born in Bethlehem

I thought as a boy that there could be no greater life than to sing praise to God. There could be no greater life than kneeling—without pad, to be more holy—as an altar boy at the small black Episcopal church of my boyhood listening to our old Bahamian priest—all of us Bahamian-descended black folk belonged to three Episcopal churches in the city—intone in a richly accented singsongy chant from the *Book of Common Prayer:*

All glory be to thee, Almighty God, our heavenly Father, for that thou, of thy tender mercy, didst give thine only Son Jesus Christ to suffer death upon the Cross for our redemption; who made there (by his one oblation of himself once offered) a full, perfect, and sufficient sacrifice, oblation, and satisfaction, for the sins of the whole world; and did institute, and in his holy

Gospel command us to continue, a perpetual memory of that his precious death and
sacrifice until his coming again....

And the hazy, incensed, sunlit silence would
break when I had rung the bell, signaling the
transubstantiation, and I would think to myself
in that mystic moment, "O God, never let me
leave this place." Then I would look at Victor
Pettijohn—our thurifer, then our master of ceremonies—every Sunday, with his cool saintly
professionalism with the censer, with his aiding
of the priest, with his supervision of the other
acolytes and, thrilled beyond telling, beyond
ordinary measure, would just say to myself,
"Boy!" I was disappointed to learn that when
Rosalind took my *Book of Common Prayer* it
was not to read but to fill a space in her book-
shelf, as its unusual size gave her collection
symmetry. "I'm glad she's not into that voodoo
nonsense of watered-down Catholicism anyway," Ida the Baptist says, truly spoken by
someone who spent six years in a segregated
Catholic school in Dallas.

Ida, my wise counsel, is as dedicated to virtue, and to the possibilities and expressiveness
of sheer goodness, as perhaps any human being
I have ever met. She understands intuitively the
human heart. I, on the other hand, am more

conflicted, even, sometimes, confounded by such matters. But this admission about faith struggle should hardly be striking for an author who reads passages from *The Confessions of Augustine* and Bunyan's *Grace Abounding to the Chief of Sinners* nearly every week.

I doubt if my children believe anything remotely Christian. I have read significant chunks of the Bible to them, and their response is that it is a nice story but, as Rosalind put it, "Who can believe that stuff?" And Ida has been more than a little annoyed at the three of us in church, making doodles, and suffocating laughs from private jokes when the minister is delivering his sermons. "You act more like a kid than they do; you are shaming me in church," she scolded. For periods of time, I will straighten up, chastising Rosalind and Linnet for not paying attention to the sermon, for acting disruptive during the service, but this enforcement does not last long. There is something about church, its sanctified boredom, that brings out the kid in me that was suppressed when I was a kid, and I am very glad to have my children for company when I am there. In fact, I hate the idea of going without them.

"Why do the faithful go to church?" asked a Catholic priest once of Linnet when she, having a sudden urge to investigate Catholicism, went with me to a nearby Catholic church to find out about it.

"Well," said Linnet nervously, put on edge by the inquisitorial nature of the discussion, looking desperately at me for a sense of the right answer.

"Tell him why *you* go to church," I said quietly.

And she seemed at once markedly relieved by having the question placed in the personal.

"Oh, I go to church," she said, "to make friends and have a good time."

The priest thought this to be a fairly, well, lackluster answer, bordering between childishness and improper parental instruction.

"Did I give the wrong answer?" Linnet asked sheepishly when we left.

"No," I said, laughing. "That's the most sensible answer I've ever heard for joining a church."

"I mean," Linnet continued, "when the priest started talking about sacraments and catechism and all that stuff I didn't understand, I thought, well, it kinda sounded like school. I don't want to join a church if it's just like being in school. I felt maybe I wouldn't be smart enough for that religion, because I'm L.D.

I don't want to struggle and feel dumb trying to learn a religion. But would you have taken me to a Catholic church if I had wanted to go?"

"Yes," I said, "I would have gone with you for as long as you wanted to go."

"But you wouldn't have become Catholic?" she asked.

"No," I said. "But I would have supported you if that was what you really wanted to do."

So ended the adventure with Catholicism.

"I'll believe if you do," Linnet said once after I read the story of the Resurrection from Mark.

A long time passed before I answered.

"Do you believe it?" she asked again. "Do you, Daddy?"

"Yes," I said at last. "But you shouldn't believe just because I do. Don't ever say that again." And I shut the Bible and walked away from the table.

"Your children love you very much," Ida said. "They admire you. They worship the ground you walk on. You hurt them when you say something like that. You could go a long way toward making them believers. What's wrong with them believing because you do?"

"Because," I said to Ida, "I might be wrong.

I might be a hypocrite. I might be a liar. Because of all the things I know I never can be and all the base things that I know that I am, they cannot believe *through* me. Who knows? One day their relationship with me might change for the worse, and that shouldn't determine the question of their faith. Mark Twain was right when he said that if religion were truly a matter of freedom of conscience and not family conformity, then any given family should be a mixture of Christians, agnostics, Buddhists, Jews, and anything else. Rosalind and Linnet must believe on their accord and in their own way."

"Okay, but don't make this business too intellectual or too spiritual," Ida warned. "After all, the fact that you believe should mean something to them. You know that old blues song you like to play, 'You're Gonna Need Somebody on Your Bond.' People need the assurance that other people believe."

This book then is the story of a faith struggle, of how the members of a family come to believe in each other and, through this, I think, to believe in that which not only makes belief in ourselves possible, but makes it matter. Ida was right: we're all gonna need somebody on our bond. It is also a story where race, oddly, plays only a very small role; class is a great deal more important. But mostly this is a tale that turns on the mundane events of our lives: how people living together understand and support each other—even take joy in knowing each other—despite petty annoyances, blatant misunderstandings, embarrassments, ordinary but stressful trials, numerous insensitivities, moments of utter cowardice, and both inadvertent and willful ignorance.

"Do you like being a parent—you know, being a father, having children and all?" Linnet once asked me.

"Yes," I said, after a moment. "It's like dancing with a partner. It takes a lot of effort to do it well. But when it's done well it's a beautiful thing to see."

PART I

SCHOOL:
WHAT WE ARE

There is no such thing as a grown up person.
—the priest in André Malraux's
Anti-Memoirs

*Let Jogli rejoice with the Linnet, who is distinct
and of mild delight.*
—Christopher Smart, *Rejoice in
the Lamb*

TUMBLING

"You know the secret of cartwheels, Roxanne?"

"No," I said, interested, thinking there might be some secret I could learn from her, some intellectual knowledge that I could translate into body knowledge.

"Catch yourself before you kill yourself," she whispered, as she retied her sneaker. "Catch yo-self."

> —Patricia Henley, "The Secret of
> Cartwheels"

When Linnet was taking dance lessons, back when she was five, six, seven years old, she went through a period when she tried, all the time, to do cartwheels. Around and around she would go, never quite getting the hang of it. Her younger sister, Rosalind, also taking dance lessons (under great duress), was also, as it were, always to be found on her head, rear end up in the air, practicing tumbling, cartwheels, and the like. But Linnet particularly worked, without noticeable success, at doing cartwheels as if, for a certain period, her life depended on them. She often looked very funny in a way that had nothing to do with her ineptitude but rather with her poignancy. It

was a tender humor that I could not share with
her because to discover herself funny to anyone
would only cause her to cry, to think that I, like
the world, was utterly without mercy when,
of course, my laughter at Linnet's mistakes
came solely from the realm of a rich and pure
mercy. Child, why do you torment yourself so?

"Can you do a cartwheel, Daddy?" she
asked me one day.

"Nope," I answered.

"Could you do one when you were a kid?"

"Nope, never could. I could never do a cartwheel. I could never do a handstand. I could never tumble well in gym class. I was always jealous of the kids who could."

"I can't do those things either. I can't even do one chin-up."

"Couldn't do those when I was a kid either. My arms were too skinny or something. I hated chin-ups."

She was silent for a while, as if considering the meaning of all this. I myself was a bit unsure if I should have made this rash confession of physical incompetence. I thought it might bring me down a bit in her eyes if she thought her father was some sort of weakling. Perhaps that would not give her confidence, and it has always been doses of confidence, like a kind of mental medicine, an emotional elixir, that I have handed out to Linnet with the wish not of cure but of, shall we say, periods of remission.

"What's the point of doing cartwheels? Or chin-ups? Or any of that stuff that you have to do in gym class? That's what I don't like about dance class, doing cartwheels and those other things I can't do," she said, annoyed. There was much, I guessed, that she did not like about dance class. I would sometimes watch the class through the one-way looking glass and could see her, a picture of the most distressed concentration, trying her hardest to get the steps right. Because she had experienced so much failure in her young life, never was there a child who was more afraid of it, more petrified by it, more completely undone and ashamed in the face of it. I would feel deeply sorry for her when I watched her try to dance (it was one of the few times in both our lives that I actually saw her in a "learning environ-ment," as it is called) and I would feel deeply anxious for her as well. I have spent all of her school life feeling an anxiety for her that, at times, had to be as deep and unrelenting as the anxiety she felt for herself.

"Don't feel bad that you can't do some-thing," I said, suddenly breaking the silence, feeling a pep talk coming on. "After all, all that shows is that you can have a massive number of failures in this life and still turn out okay. Look at me. I turned out okay and I'm one of the most inept, incompetent, ignorant persons I know. When you're young you waste a lot of time trying to do stuff you cannot possibly do but it bothers you that you can't do it. When you're older, you keep doing it, but it doesn't matter whether you get it right or not. You don't get bothered if it's not right. If you use failure right, it can save your life, maybe. Life is mostly failing at something. You learn not to mind it."

She looked at me, nearly in tears. "But I *do* mind it *now.*" And she went back to trying cartwheels.

Adventures at School

"When I was in grade school," I told Linnet, one rainy afternoon when she was, I think, in third grade and trying hopelessly to learn the multiplication tables, "the teachers didn't mind roughing you up if you didn't learn your lessons. Most of the teachers I had were black and at that time it was considered appropriate to spank kids, to whip them, especially black kids, in order to keep them in line. You know the old saying, 'Spare the rod and spoil the child.' So I grew up in that. When I had to learn my multiplication tables in the fourth grade, the teacher would have us sit in a circle and she would drill us with flash cards. If you didn't know the answer, you were smacked on the hand with a ruler. I was terribly afraid, so I memorized these tables as if my life depended on it. But as you can see, it proved an effective way to learn multiplication. You've got it easy now. Nobody slaps you around. These teachers you have today are very soft. They pass out praise as if it were a narcotic and have very little understanding of what you need—"

"Did you like getting slapped around in school?" she asked bluntly, interrupting me through her tears, as she always cried when she and I worked at her studies in those days.

I was silent for several moments, as if I were trying very much to measure an answer that would have the proper sort of parental weight to it. But actually, at that moment, I was recalling with almost crushing immediacy one afternoon when my elementary school gym teacher slapped me viciously across the head because he thought I had been whispering in line. I wanted very much to cry but could not in sight of the other children. But I felt, at the moment, the wretched cruelty of this arbitrary justice (for I was not the person who was whispering) and the deep humiliation of this harsh authority. "Adults beat you up because they're bigger," a boy told me during my youth. "When you become an adult and you're as big as they are, they won't bother you anymore." I wonder how many children I grew up with fantasized about not being children but being adults because adults, it seemed, had, if not power precisely, at least the sheer stature and presence to enforce the possibility of being left alone.

I looked at Linnet's tear-streaked face and thought that it was a great deal like my own face at that age. Linnet is a child who, it must be admitted, looks a great deal like her father: tear-stained, sullen, shy, lacking confidence, inept at pleasing, the epitome of dullness. I, too, was a dull, completely undistinguished child. I sighed and gave up the effort of being parental.

"No," I said matter-of-factly, "I never liked getting slapped around and I never liked school. Not a single day of it. It felt just like prison. I couldn't wait to get out."

"Neither can I," she said with finality.

FIRST POEM FOR LINNET

Linnet was seven years old when I wrote my first poem for her. I was then a visiting professor at the University of Kansas on a minority postdoctoral fellowship. I would make the five-hour trip from Lawrence, Kansas, to St. Louis every weekend, for Ida and the girls did not go with me. The first several months were not a partic-

ularly good time between Ida and me, though
Linnet and Rosalind did not notice it. We have
always kept them sheltered from any sense of
tension or undercurrent of disruption that may
occur in the normal course of a marriage. This
was intensely important to the both of us: the
girls must not grow up in a bickering, conten-
tious atmosphere. Only once do I remember
either Linnet or Rosalind overhearing an argument between me and Ida. Linnet was, I think,
two, and Ida and I were arguing about in-laws
or money or the quest for social status, frequent
topics of disagreement during the early years of
our marriage. It had become so heated that
Linnet, who was in the bathroom working at
her "potty training," emerged, training pants
down, face distressed, shouting: "What going
on? I want to know! What going on?" So hilarious and so touching it was, that the argument
was instantly tabled. It was during these early
months in Lawrence (I wound up staying there
on the fellowship for two years) that Ida once,
rather angrily, almost as if on a dare, asked me
to have the children in Lawrence one weekend
instead of my coming home.

"But that's crazy," I said. "You'd have to
drive up here to drop them off on Thursday
and come for them on Sunday."

"I want a weekend to myself," she said, sternly.

So, for that weekend, the children stayed with me in my tiny efficiency.

"Yeah, Daddy, I remember that real well," said Linnet recently. "You slept on the floor and Ros and I slept on your Murphy bed. You cooked for us in this tiny, tiny kitchen. And we watched the PBS children's programs on a black-and-white TV that you had. That was the first time I ever watched a black-and-white TV. We went for walks in the park, to the library. And you couldn't comb our hair right. You kept trying to get it into these barrettes and they kept popping loose, so that, by the end of the day, our hair was all over the place. And you kept muttering, when you were combing our hair, 'How do women do this stuff?' You combed our hair real soft, like you were afraid of hurting us or something, and Ros kept saying, 'Comb harder, Daddy, it's not tight enough.' That was a great weekend, one of the best I ever had."

Because I was alone much of the time while I was in Lawrence, I was able to do a great deal of writing, mostly essays, but also many poems. I thought of making Linnet the subject of an essay, but I could not quite get my mind around the matter. I could not then come to terms with how to write about her in prose. I had written an essay while in Lawrence entitled "Waiting for Miss America" in which both Linnet and Rosalind were mentioned, but they were not the subject of the essay. I had to grow more to learn how to write about them, especially Linnet. In those early years, I did not understand my children, or fully comprehend parenthood, except that, naturally, I was supposed to love my children, which I believe I did, although I was not in any way sure what it was that I was loving. I also felt guilty and deeply uncomfortable whenever I momentarily disliked them. But the poem for Linnet was meant to be a kind of shorthand, a mental place holder to say, "Come back to this when you are older and she is as well." I wrote it one night on a Montgomery Ward electric typewriter after I had written a rough draft in longhand on my knees with the pad on the bed (a favorite writing position at that time). I did not show it to Linnet for nearly two years; that is, she saw it for the first time when she was probably nine years old. I was afraid she would misunderstand what I wanted to say and, after all, frankly, perhaps I was not at all sure what I was trying to say beneath it all. It had been published nearly a year before I showed it to her. She read it slowly.

"It's nice," she said when finished. "I don't understand it all but I like it. It sounds nice. It sounds like it's about you and me when we take walks together."

She thought for a moment, then asked suddenly, "Why did you write it?"

"There was," I responded, "something I wanted to say to you. I couldn't figure out any other way to say it. I was afraid to show it to you because I thought you might not like a poem about your being slow."

"What's it matter?" she said off-handedly. "Everybody knows I'm dumb."

The pain I felt at that admission was both bitter and deep.

"You're not dumb," I said.

"You got mad at me once and called me dumb," she said.

I hung fire briefly. "If I ever said that to you, I am sorry. But I don't remember ever calling you that. I don't call people names."

"You thought it," she said, looking down.

"If I have ever thought that," I said, "then I am more sorry than words can say."

I have read this poem publicly only once. The occasion was in the spring of 1988, shortly after I had been tenured at Washington University. Jim McLeod, then the chair of African and Afro-American Studies, wanted me to read some poems before a gathering of black students. I did not want to do this as I have always felt a bit uncomfortable doing readings. Moreover, I sensed that the sort of stuff I had written was not likely to impress the students. It wasn't Afrocentric. It wasn't Nikki Giovanni. It wasn't even strikingly good poetry. But I agreed to do it as Jim is a dear colleague. At the last minute I decided to take Linnet with me to the reading.

"This is exciting," she said. "I never heard you read before."

I read for probably twenty minutes and, on impulse, ended with "Dumbo's Ears." I explained to the audience that Linnet was learning disabled and I wrote this poem for her. I am not sure why I decided to read it at all, perhaps to give some reason for bringing my daughter, perhaps to see how she would respond to having her "problem" publicly exposed. I think at that stage in our relationship I was trying to find out something about myself, trying to find out, actually, if I was more deeply bothered by Linnet's learning disability than I had ever been willing to admit to myself, by trying to deal with Linnet's problem publicly. I wanted to understand what being a good parent was, and perhaps there are moments in the relationship when this can be best understood only in some sort of public ritual, some public display. Linnet, in any case, seemed not even to be listening. She was rocking back and forth on a piano bench, making faces, seemingly in her own world. I was a bit horrified by her behavior, reminding me, as it did, of the senseless rocking of a retarded boy I knew in my neighborhood as a child. God, I thought, these people are likely to think she is retarded or something. Why can't she sit there, prim and proper, and listen? They'll think I have an idiot for a daughter. I felt that spasm of shame that she had made me feel so much in the past, and the shame of that shame. I also felt a moment of true annoyance with her. She had let me down as she had several times before, but I instantly felt bad about feeling that way. Am I ever to be worthy of this girl? I thought. She deserves someone so much better as a father than I.

When I finished the poem, I felt, oddly, disarmingly almost, a sense of relief and a fierce sense of pride. Perhaps it was merely a kind of disingenuous public defiance, a public show of wanting to be the good parent, the caring, protective father. But that was only a part of it. This is my daughter, I thought, and I will never disown her for what she is or is not. Whether this was driven entirely by a kind of "audience egotism," it was nonetheless a proper way to feel, the way Linnet deserved to have her father feel. I thought of Augustine's words: I do this for love of your love. I looked at her rocking there, caught her eye, and grinned. Before me sat the image of my own face.

"As a boy," I told her once, "I was called 'Happy.' The other boys called me 'Happy' and it became my nickname when I was about eight years old. I was furious about it at first and I would yell at the boys not to call me that. How dare they give me a name I did not want or like? I was outraged. Besides, it was a degrading name. It was the name of a local TV program called *Happy the Clown*. I hated the name but it stuck for several years, until I was about fourteen."

"Why did they call you that?" Linnet asked.

"Because I was very shy as a boy and people always thought I was sad. But I wasn't really. I was just self-absorbed. I had a sad face just like yours. You know the way everyone says you have a sad face. I had the same face as a child, so the boys thought it would be funny to call me 'Happy.'"

"I hate people thinking you're sad when you're not. I get that all the time. 'Are you unhappy, Linnet?' 'Why are you sad, Linnet?' And I'm not sad. I'm feeling just fine. I wish people would just leave my face alone, stop treating my face like it's their property."

I looked at her when I finished the poetry reading and made the only gesture I could, the one gesture I felt she would appreciate. I threw my arm around her shoulder and we walked out together without another word or even a good-bye.

"Thank you, Daddy, for taking me," she said. "I liked it, especially the last poem."

"Did it make you uncomfortable?" I asked. "I mean, reading that poem? Maybe I shouldn't have read it."

"I'm glad you read it," she said, smiling. "It sounded real good. I thought you read it just for me. Besides, I was real proud. How many of those college kids can say their dads write poems about them and can read them in front of people?"

Dumbo's Ears or How We Begin

(FOR LINNET, MY DAUGHTER)

there is always talk among the knowing kind
If you are last to do a certain thing or anything or
    everything

that you are a slow one, as slow as the time
it takes to say anything twice or more

that you helplessly do not see the plainest
sights to be seen anywhere by anybody plainly

that you are as ungainly as Dumbo's ears, as
clumsy as a childish elephant with floppy ears

but there's always been a kind of pleasure
in a certain kind of slowness like a gait

that sort of ambles a bit through the park
or shuffles along the street sort of stopping

and not quite knowing where it's going because
what with stones and leaves and silver rabbits

and silken insects and all manner of infinite trash
and voices and echoes and signs and the wide sky

well, who could really help but be subverted
    in one's quickness
if one is really a sky lover and likes to watch
    the earth too

so there is no real reason to go anywhere in
    particular
except the somewhere that anywhere can lead
    easily

along some way or other until another more
outright way comes, a way that is more a gift

that would make the gait even slower and
    more stately
like a meandering stream's or a balloon ascent

or a blues saxophone or the words of a
    wedding or
the reading of any text worth the wait or water

evaporating in a glass—all a kind of awful
    slowness
that seems, like our gait together, to say *wait
    awhile*

and which, like the whiling tortoise, always starts
    the race
after the quick and the hares, gate open, in their
    blind rush, begin

"God be gracious to the winners"

It was not uncommon in the early days of Linnet's schooling, before Ida and I understood or even knew of her learning disability, for me to make speeches, give impassioned lectures to her about her repeated failures in school. In retrospect, these speeches must have convinced her that I was either a theatrical lunatic or an arrogant race man. The only time, with perhaps one or two exceptions, I ever talked about race in my household, made a point of race pride or racial identification, was during these lectures. I am sure that it was all a reflection of my own insecurity, my own anxiety about the white world in which I found myself living, in which I found her being educated. I was not only embarrassed *for* her, but for a long time I was probably embarrassed *by* Linnet. At night, in our bedroom, when Linnet was asleep (or at least we thought she was asleep; one wonders how many of these conversations she actually may have overheard), I would sometimes go into nearly uncontrollable rages with Ida:

"Linnet wants pity from her white teachers. She has to be stronger than that. I can't stand that. I can't stand the idea of accepting pity from anyone. It shows you're weak. I especially cannot stand accepting pity from a white person, for being dumb," I would say angrily to Ida.

"I cannot understand how a person who can be as kind as you can be," Ida would respond, "goes off the deep end about this. You sound like a crazy man whenever we talk about Linnet's schooling. First, you say you don't care what she does in school, that school is unimportant. Then, you talk about her not being strong enough, that she seeks the pity and comfort of the white teachers in her school, plays upon her weaknesses so that they will feel sorry for her. You want her to hold school in the utter disdain that you do, yet you also want her to do well, because, to your mind, that's the best way to hold school in disdain."

"You cannot show yourself as weak, especially if you're black, especially in front of whites. I can't stand the idea of anyone, especially a white person, feeling sorry for me. Linnet must adopt the same attitude. All they see in her is a dumb, black kid," I would shout.

"You're crazy," Ida would say, exasperated.

"Why? Because I don't want to have a weak kid, because I want her to have pride for herself, for her—"

"Don't say 'race,' because this has nothing to do with race. It's deeper and more personal than that with you. It has to do with your own childhood, your own rearing. There is something puritanical and harsh in you. You value endurance and forbearing above anything else. Race pride? Are you kidding? You're suffering from race inferiority, from the John Henry syndrome, from the 'I gotta show the white folks I'm better than they are' blues. I don't want my child infected with your nuttiness."

"John Henry syndrome? Well, what's wrong with that? There could be worse models than that."

"Not really," Ida would say, rolling over in bed, turning out her lamp and pulling the covers up. "You see what happened to him. You keep acting like that, I don't expect you to live too long. When are you going to learn that nobody has to prove anything to anybody out here? When are you going to learn that character is not built on stoicism and certainly not on bitterness?"

It would do very little if I were to tell Linnet now that I am deeply ashamed of the shame I felt then, some of which was rooted in my reaction to her. On another level, though, it was not directly attached to her. I felt a shame for

myself, my blackness, that manifested itself as
a kind of perverse strength, or a bitter deter-
mination to prove myself. I think shame often
winds up being expressed in people as odd
forms of strength or excessive pride. My
mother was a strong woman who felt great
skepticism, utter disdain, about the idea of
needing other people, of having other people,
whether black or white, think that they ever
had done or ever could do anything for her. I
am sure that this insistent independence found
its source in some well of shame. But, in her situation, this probably made her a more effective
parent by giving her a sense of more control
over a decidedly precarious life. Having inher-
ited something of that pride, it has made me, in
my very different situation, many times, a
lesser parent, less understanding, less patient,
less forgiving of myself or anyone else. What
was a nobility in my mother expresses itself
often in me as a neurosis. For a long time, I
wanted Linnet to have this same strength,
which meant that she had to have the shame
that was the source of the strength. I could not
understand that she was as different from me
as I was from my mother.

But it has been the years of Linnet's schooling, very difficult years for us all, that have

made me aware of one inescapable yet largely unnoticed fact: namely, that fatherhood, my own obsession with relation, was not a role at all but rather a mask or, even more accurately put, a series of masks. I could be, I discovered, by turns stern, loving, wise, silly, youthful, aged, racial, universal, indulgent, strict, with a remarkably easy and often cunning detachment that led me to the question of not whether I loved my children but what sort of love there is between a parent and a child, at last. And for her part, I wonder now what Linnet must have thought, then, and what she thinks now, of these masks, dropped and put in place so adeptly, whether she sees her father not quite as a human being, but rather as a series of personifications of adult moods, of various ways that an adult, spurred by guilt, by annoyance, by condescension, by loneliness, deals with the prerogatives of power and love.

"Are you glad you had me?" Linnet asked once.

"I cannot live without you," I respond with sincere heartfelt expression, with real thanksgiving for this loving child; it is for both of us, however, a cunningly manipulative evasion.

❖

Linnet was born on the afternoon of September 14, 1979, at Tompkins County Hospital in Ithaca, New York. I was then a graduate student in English at Cornell University and my wife was working as a secretary for the Africana Studies Center there. It was a hard birth, a very long labor, for Linnet was nearly a breech baby (and three weeks beyond the due date). The doctor had to use forceps. For a time there was such a worried look on his face that I feared for both Ida and the child. But everything ended on the very rainy afternoon in a kind of shimmer of love and good fortune. Linnet was born and for a long time, perhaps thirty minutes, Ida and I, with baby Linnet, were left entirely alone in the delivery room. She made no sound at all, curled like a young, strange animal, indecipherable in its innocence, as unused to the world as we were unused to the sight of her. Ida seemed tired and relieved and aglow with a sense of the miraculous: herself a miracle, the child a miracle, and the moment a wonder-working—utterly dazzling and completely commonplace. The rain fell heavily.

Linnet was slow at doing everything—at walking, at talking, at potty training, the latter an especially disastrous period. Ida and I, probably reading some child-rearing book, had tried to train Linnet too early. The accidents, frequent and messy, doubtless willful as well at times, tried my patience more than they should. I somehow thought something was at stake here, that Linnet's mastery of this was more to me than my sense of her well-being. I am not completely sure why being a parent in those early years felt, at moments, like such an utterly pressurized experience. Months went by without success. Linnet cried and cried. Suddenly, at about twenty-eight months, she caught on. It was as though Ida and I had taught her nothing; she taught herself when she was ready to learn it. A long and unhappy time passed before I understood the lesson embedded here.

Shortly after Linnet's second birthday, her sister, Rosalind, was born and we all moved to St. Louis because I had been offered a job in the Black Studies Program at Washington University. Another phase in our lives began, although it is so seamless to the children who, because they were so young when we moved, were under the impression for some time that they were born in St. Louis. It was Ida's idea that Linnet should attend the Wilson School, a private school in Clayton, Missouri, when she was four. I am not sure why Ida was so emphatic about this: part of the reason was that

Linnet was being baby-sat in a home that made both of us uneasy. Some black women in the poorer part of town were running this operation in the dark, unfinished basement of their home. Linnet hated it but never refused to go. She just looked unhappy once she was there and was overjoyed to see us when we came for her. Wilson School seemed a bad idea to me, mostly for the expense. We were hardly in a position to be able to afford a high-class private school. I was also worried about Linnet's slowness, which was already plain to us. But Ida convinced me that the school would be better than another year at the baby-sitter: the environment was better and we would worry less. Besides, how could we be sure she was really slow? She had never been in school.

As it turned out, we worried more for the one year Linnet was at Wilson School than we did when she went to the baby-sitter. Of all her years of schooling, this was, without question, the worst for her. It confirmed our fears as well. Her teachers told us during parent conferences that she could not count to ten, did not know her colors, could not properly hold a pencil, could not properly cut paper with scissors, had defective large motor and small motor skills, was immature for her age, could not follow simple directions, and seemed generally incapable of learning. "But she is such a nice, well-behaved child," they said. "She's very sweet."

"Listen," I said to Ida one night, "this Wilson School stuff is crazy. I'm paying good money I can't afford to have these teachers tell me that I've got a stupid kid. Their attitude is that she isn't quite human or quite worthy of respect because she isn't gifted like the other kids or academically talented or whatever. Let's get her the hell out of that pretentious hellhole."

"We've sunk too much money in this," Ida responded. "We can't take her out. She has to stick it out. It might get better as she adjusts."

"It's not going to get any better," I exploded. "I don't want her there being reminded in a hundred and fifty different ways every day that she's dumb. I can't stand that. I can't stand the school anyway and those conceited parents that send their kids there, with their Volvos with the college sticker in the back and all that nonsense."

"Are you mad just because you've got no money and can't drive a Volvo yourself? I didn't think there were any greater snobs in America than the Early family of Philadelphia. Your people think they're better than everybody."

"No, I'm mad because I'm tired of snobs

with their 'precious,' 'gifted' kids. They remind me of the snobs who went to my church, the light-skinned middle-class blacks. They thought I was dirt, because my family was dark-skinned and had no money. They're all cut from the same cloth. They are obsessed with status. Is that the reason you're sending her to this school, for status? Is that the reason we had a big birthday party for her this year, because you did not wish to be outdone by the other parents who had thrown big parties for their children?"

"Sometimes," Ida sighed, "you can just get plain irrational. Linnet's going to school has nothing to do with slights from your childhood. That attitude doesn't help Linnet. The problem here is not my middle-class pretensions."

I laid my head on the kitchen table and Ida held my arm. I looked up at Ida, despairingly. "Why can't she learn, Ida? Why can't she just be normal and do the stuff in school? Is she retarded? Did we do something to her to make her like this?"

Actually, Linnet's departure from the school became a moot point that fall when one day she twice made bowel movements on herself. Then, a few days later she made another. She was under so much stress and was so nervous in school that I think she just, at moments, lost control of herself. When I came to school after the second incident, her teacher said, "I really don't know if Linnet is ready to be here." Linnet had been crying hysterically but had calmed herself a bit upon my arrival. Once inside the car she began to cry wildly again.

"Hush," I said irritably. "It's over and done with and crying certainly won't do you or the situation much good. So just hush!"

I gave her a tissue and she tried to pull herself together, her chest heaving, her lips trembling.

"I'm...sorry, Daddy. I...know you hate me." She could barely get the words out, she stammered so much.

I leaned my head against the steering wheel for a moment. "I don't hate you, Linnet. I just don't want you to hate yourself. It's over and done with. Now, you mustn't let it happen again. You must be a big girl now because you're going to school. And big girls don't make bowel movements on themselves."

"Okay," she hiccupped.

Briefly, I felt this urge, nearly choking in its intensity, to embrace her, to hold her, to comfort her, to tell her the story about when I wet myself in the second grade, in front of the whole class, while we were singing the national anthem, because I was too afraid to tell the teacher I had to go to the bathroom.

When I was a boy, my mother never told me a single story about her childhood: what it was like to grow up in a family of so many children or to have a Bahamian father or how she met my father or how they fell in love or why she quit high school or what she liked to do as a child. There was a great air of seriousness and purpose about my mother, and I think she thought that to indulge in such memory recitation was sentimental and childish. There was only the immediate concern of survival, of keeping her family together and out of trouble and getting all of us through school, with clothes on our backs, food in our mouths, a few books, and some pinch of dignity. And my mother's outsized matriarchal authority both intimidated and awed me, inspired me, yet, in some ways, estranged me from her. I would have liked for her to tell me when I was a boy those many personal things about herself. So often I wanted to ask but was afraid. Consequently, I grew up thinking my mother to be something a great deal more than a real person, and, in that respect, unapproachable on some levels. So I suppressed this urge to comfort and confess immediately, as my mother would have done, muttering to myself, "That won't do Linnet any good and she wouldn't understand anyway." I was to get over this and eventually share my childhood with my children. Indeed, stories of my childhood became, for them and for me, the very thread of continuity and love, of identification and convergence, that structured our relationship. But in the early years I was very much my mother's child. She was, it must be remembered, all I knew about parenting.

My demeanor as a parent perfectly mimicked my mother's. She was neither sympathetic nor affectionate when I was a boy. Whenever I would cry, she would always tell me to hush, that crying never solved anything. Whenever she combed my hair, I wanted very much to cry because it hurt a great deal. She said I was, as the black folk put it, "tender-headed," and would simply grab my head and tell me to "be still." Then she would relentlessly grease and brush my hair until it felt as if it were on fire. I suppose this small act, this duty I am sure she found to be a headache, had something to do with the pressure she was under in rearing three children by herself, with the peculiar social stress of rearing a boy in a way that he might be able to function in the society with some sense of confidence, with the constraint of having no money. "So much of what we as black people are," wrote actor Sidney Poitier, "has to do directly with the fact that our forefathers were not able to pass on the good life to us." My mother certainly knew that she could not pass on any sort of good life to me. "You have to be a man," she would say, "and learn to take care of yourself in this world." And my response to Linnet, its lack of empathy, of tenderness, may very well have been my own fear of being unable—insecure, tenuously positioned professional that I was then—to pass the good life on to Linnet, and wanting to make sure, as my mother did, that if I could not, she might be able to find it herself. I cannot be soft because it will make her soft, I thought, and soft black children cannot survive in this world. I do not know if this is true, but it was (and is) for me an undying truism.

I was fingering an American flag, an old one, with just forty-eight stars. It had been used to drape the coffin of my father, who died of a brain tumor at the age of thirty-two. My mother, a few days earlier when she visited me in St. Louis, had given me all that he left: this flag (a result of a military burial), a death certificate, a few books including a first edition of

Jack Johnson's autobiography, induction papers. She told me that he had told her about some German prisoners he had talked to while he was in the army during World War II. The Germans asked him why he was fighting for a country that so brutally mistreated his people. "Why are you fighting for white people in a white man's war?" they asked. He was permitted to be only a cook in a segregated army. "I couldn't answer them," he told my mother. "I wanted to but I couldn't say anything. I guess they were right, but I hope it will be better for my children than it was for me." That was all, the sum total of a life and an inheritance.

"I want to give my children something more than this," I said to Ida as she took the flag and other items from me and put them in a box.

"What do you remember about your year at Wilson School?" I asked Linnet a few months ago.

"Nothing much," she said. "I had two women teachers. There was a block corner there and I liked to play in it. I didn't have any friends as I remember. And I read a book that I really liked about a caterpillar who kept eating things and getting bigger and bigger. I can't remember the name but it was a great book. Why do you ask? What do you think I would remember?"

"I don't know. It wasn't a good year for you. It was your first year in school and it was pretty tough."

"Because of the L.D.?" she asked.

"Yes, but also because I don't think you were ready for school just then."

"Why did you send me?"

"We couldn't help it," I said simply.

She looked a little perplexed by that response but just shrugged her shoulders. "Well, it's behind me now."

THE (UN) HAPPIEST I'VE BEEN

"The worst day I had at school was in kindergarten at the Old Bonhomme School," Linnet told me one day recently. "We were all told to come to school dressed in some crazy way because we had just read that book, *Wacky Wednesday*. And the day we were coming to school like that was a Wednesday. I forgot about it and I was the only kid in the class dressed all right. I just cried and cried the whole day. I felt like such a fool being the only kid without crazy clothes. I don't know why. I just did."

"Linnet, why didn't you just put your shoes on the wrong feet? That would have been a little crazy," Rosalind offered.

"I'm L.D., remember? My shoes were probably already on the wrong feet."

"The happiest day I had at school was in the sixth grade," Rosalind said to me, "when it snowed like crazy and every other school district in St. Louis had the day off but Webster Groves. Well, most of the kids didn't go but because I have such great parents who are so concerned that I get an education, I was right there. It was such a great day! Most of the building was empty. I could find a seat on the school bus. The teachers let you play games in class. Even gym class was pretty okay, and you know how I hate gym. I loved being at school when nobody was there. That day was, without a doubt, the happiest I've been."

A Day at School for Rosalind (from Rosalind's diary, verbatim)

November 1, 1992

In my last entry I really didn't make myself clear who I was and who I'm talking about. Well for one thing my name is Rosalind Early. I'm in 6th grade it's the pits! The highlight of the day really is reading. I have a nice teacher Mrs. R (that took me a few weeks to learn to spell and say) and a pretty nice class. 2 of my friends are in it. The part of the day I hate is Social Studies. Mr. L talks a lot (Oh, Mr. L's the teacher) and is boring. School is okay it's not exactly the pits but Mr. L needs shaping up and how! At my school we just completed the space program. The whole school built this space lab, on Friday we took it down. I didn't exactly enjoy the space program and I didn't get to paint or work on the Bubble at all! But I did learn a lot about space!!! Like different kinds of energy and about how a rocket takes off.

Second Poem for Linnet

> *...and all hearts*
> *Were chilled into a selfish prayer for light:*
> *And they did live by watchfires...*
>
> —Lord Byron, "Darkness"

Linnet suffered her most severe social ostra-
cism from the third through the sixth grade. By
this time she had been diagnosed as learning
disabled and was assigned to the Resource
Room with a special-education teacher for certain periods every day. She hated this as it
meant that all the world knew her as a
dummy—although kindergarten and first and
second grades were so miserable, so disheart-
ening, that I suspect most of the kids thought
she was a dummy even before the trips to the
Resource Room—and other children, the
smart kids Linnet wanted to hang out with,
wanted nothing to do with her.

For a good portion of this time, Linnet and
Rosalind wore short Afro hairstyles. I am not
quite sure how this came about, although I do
know it ostensibly had to do with their taking
swim lessons and the necessity, because of that,
to have hairstyles that were easy to manage,
that they could take care of themselves. But

also at this time Linnet started coming home talking about wanting hair that could blow in the breeze, hair she could fling as she saw the white girls in school doing. This annoyed me terrifically although I pretended to ignore it, not that I was exactly angry at Linnet; I was more upset at being at the mercy of the dumb habits and conceits of white people. Or, as a relative of mine once put it, "living with white folk is no hardship, but it can have its annoyances." (Yet I think, in the end, that Linnet's desire to get her hair straightened had little to do with politics, although I must admit that I was glad, very proud as an African American, that they wore Afros. There was something about it that appealed to me racially and I thought they were adorable, cute as buttons when they had them. My one small bout of racial chauvinism was seeing my daughters in Afros. I took more photos of them during those years than at any other time before or since. But my instincts, in regard to women's beauty styles, were not entirely trustworthy and I never wanted my children to wear their hair for me.

"Do you have to write about the time when we had the Afros?" Linnet complained. "That was the worst time of my life. I hated that hairstyle and school was really going bad then. Can't you just skip it?"

"But I've already written about it," I said.

"When?" Linnet asked.

"A few years ago in some essays called 'Life with Daughters.' You remember, don't you?"

"Yeah," Linnet said slowly, "yeah, I remember. Okay, fine. So why write about it again?"

"It's part of the story. It'll be just fine, you'll see," I said, trying to soothe.

"Yeah, sure," she said disgustedly. "I'll be glad when I can write my own books about myself.")

But what undoubtedly made this hair change more difficult for both the girls and me was that Ida had, almost at the same time, changed her hairstyle from an Afro to straightened hair. This happened during a difficult time in our marriage. Ida, who had worn an Afro for the entire time I had known her, since undergraduate school when we were all "black and terrible," seemed almost to be announcing herself as a different person, as if one phase of our relationship and one phase of her life had ended. It took a very long time for me to get used to that, as if a dear friend had gone away, never to return. Linnet and Rosalind probably would have found it a bit easier to wear Afros if their mother had continued to wear hers, but this period became, without question, a major epoch in their childhood although it did not last very long. During the Afro period, they were taunted in school by both black and white students. For Linnet it was especially hard for she was now not only dumb but ugly as well. I gave many pep talks during those years when Linnet would come home crying, which was fairly often. There were long walks in the park, endless joke telling, stories about my own childhood, anything to brace her up. But I had a sense of extraordinary helplessness during this period, accompanied by a strange, some- times giddy, mixture of fatigue and panic. There was nothing I could do to make things easier or to change things for her. After long talks with her teachers, Ida and I discovered that there was little that they could do either. Yet Linnet never failed to go to school. Indeed, she often wanted to go when she was sick, act- ing as if she were afraid to stop going even for a moment for fear that she would lose some secret sense of momentum, some inner mecha- nism that propelled her to go on. There was a certain Becketian doggedness in her that, at times, seemed like a mulish heroism.

Because her intelligence-test scores were in a normal range, it was difficult for Linnet to be diagnosed as learning disabled and deserving of special educational services. Yet she was behind grade level in virtually every category of learning, understood little of what was said in class, and spent hours, an entire evening, doing homework that would have taken a non-learning-disabled child perhaps an hour.

"You know, Daddy," she said to me recently, "I never had recess in the first or second grades because I had to stay in and do all the class work I was behind on. I was always so behind everything in school. I kept working and working and working and I could never catch up."

"But once you were diagnosed as learning disabled you were able to go to recess?" I asked.

"Yeah," she sighed, "some. But I was still behind because I still had to keep up with my regular classes even when I was out at the Resource Room. And the first year that I went to the Resource Room, I was messing up because I couldn't tell time, so I kept missing the time I was supposed to go there or the time I was supposed to go back to my regular teacher. But it helped. I got to take recess more."

Once we received the diagnosis, Ida spent many hours reading books on learning disabilities: *Academic and Developmental Learning Disabilities; New Approaches to Learning Dis-*

abilities: Cognitive, Metacognitive, and Holistic; Learning Disabilities: Theories, Diagnosis, and Teaching Strategies; and *Handbook for Parents of Children with Learning Disabilities.* Titles like that. When Ida offered to share them with me, I declined:

"I'm already reading books by half-intelligent, overeducated professionals who fling around jargon. I don't need any of that stuff."

"Listen," Ida said sharply, "you can be flip if you want to. But I thought you might want to learn something to help your daughter."

"I'm not going to help her," I replied just as sharply, "by reading that garbage and wasting a lot of time."

"And how do you know it's garbage if you haven't read the books, Mr. Omniscience?"

"Because you haven't told me one thing you've learned from those books that you thought would help. If you had learned something, you would have told me."

What Ida did learn, however, was that few girls have learning disabilities and that most learning disabilities are associated with a behavior disorder. But Linnet was one of the most well-behaved children in her school and, as far as I could judge, one of the most articulate as well. (She often fooled people about her learning disability—and still does—because when she is relaxed, she speaks so well.) Her problem was not an inability to pay attention or some sort of hyperactivity. She has, as we learned, an academic learning disability—in other words, just a general slowness in learning most things. And as is the case with this sort of learning disability, it is possible to teach Linnet something one day and find out that she has completely forgotten it the next day, even the next hour, as if she had never been introduced to it.

"But how can you forget what I told you about subtraction yesterday? We went over this and you understood it then. What's wrong with you?" I could feel my voice rising with frustration. "Why can't you remember something as simple as that for one day?"

"I don't know, Daddy," she would yell, crying, completely distraught. "I don't know! I don't know! I'm trying but I just can't remember. I don't know why. Daddy, I'm sorry. I'm trying as hard as I can."

Yet, for other things, Linnet has a prodigious memory. She can remember events, places we've been to, what people have said to her, television shows, books she has read, movie stars, the rules and their variants of every board game she has, that I was cross with her two weeks ago on a Monday about her inability to spell the easiest words that we had gone over.

As with most L.D. kids, she also has had motor-skill problems and what is called in the jargon a social-skills deficit—that is, an inability to consistently judge what is appropriate to say in a social situation.

Ida decided that it was necessary to bring in a new phalanx of professionals to augment the set that Linnet was already dealing with. We hired tutors (who effected some good), took her to a child psychologist to help her learn how to make friends (this did no good at all). We even attended meetings of a support group at the local library whose slogan was, I think, "Advocate for Your Child/Make Your Child Her Own Best Advocate." But this entire stage of "cure," so to speak, both dismayed and bored me. I felt, for a considerable time, removed from Linnet, alienated, as if I no longer had to deal personally with her problems because now I had a group of intercessors to handle them for me.

As part of the normalizing aspect of this "cure," Linnet took piano lessons for perhaps a year with indifferent results. (Actually, I started giving both of them lessons but Ida thought I was not a good teacher, particularly because I lost my patience with Linnet, who could not seem to grasp the simplest bits, could not even remember, from week to week, where middle C was. So, in came the professional.)

"I told you not to give that child piano lessons," I said one evening after her piano teacher informed us that Linnet was doing very poorly and that it was a waste of money to continue. "Music is too abstract for her to handle. Now you've just saddled her with another failure."

"Listen, I don't want to hear any 'I told you so.' How was I to know that she couldn't learn the piano until she started taking the lessons? Besides, she ought to be treated like her sister and not as something abnormal. If Rosalind is taking lessons, Linnet should take them too. She has to be exposed to things like anyone else. How do you know what she can do until you have her try it? The way you talk, you wouldn't have her doing anything."

"That's not true," I said, feeling somewhat put upon. "I just believe in having her do projects where the chance of success is very high."

"And what are those?" Ida asked. "What are those? What she already knows how to do?"

"I was glad not to have to take those piano lessons," Linnet said recently about the matter. "I was relieved. It was just one less thing to be stressed out about. I could come home and relax instead of hearing you guys harp about practicing my lessons."

Throughout this whole period, Rosalind too was having a difficult time of it.

"You love Linnet more than you love me," Rosalind would say, nearly once a month.

"We love you both the same," I would habitually reply.

"No you don't. She gets tutors. And you and Mommy are always worried about her. You don't worry about me. You don't worry about what I do in school."

It was true that since the day Rosalind started school, performing remarkably well, Ida and I paid little attention to her or her studies. We were relieved, judging by Rosalind's abilities, that we did not have two L.D. children, so we left it at that.

"Listen," I would say, "your sister has a learning problem. So, she needs extra help. We would do the same for you if you had her problem. You're lucky that you don't have it. But we love you both the same."

"But I'm not a genius. I have problems learning some things. I can't learn everything well. So, I'm sure I need a tutor for something."

"Rosalind, please," I would say, and go

about doing something to signal the end of the conversation.

Then there was the sibling rivalry and Rosalind's discovery of a way to wound her sister.

"You're stupid, Linnet," Rosalind would shout during one of their frequent fights. "You're just plain stupid. You can't even add two plus two. You need five teachers to teach you how to read. You're stupid. And I never want to play with you again."

"Don't call me stupid," Linnet would scream, almost like someone demented. "I'm not stupid! I'm not stupid!" Often, this would be followed by a punch or a kick and Rosalind's shouting, "Don't hit me! Don't hit me!" or "She's hitting me, Daddy! She's hitting me, Daddy!"

And then I would tell Rosalind not to call her sister stupid, that it hurt her feelings, to which Rosalind would respond, "What about my feelings? All you guys ever preach to me about is her feelings. How she has L.D. and we can't hurt her feelings. Well, I have feelings. She hurts my feelings, she calls me names, but nobody says anything. I didn't give her L.D. I didn't make her dumb. Why should everything be put on me like it's my fault?"

But it was also during these crucial years of

the Afro and the "cure" when Linnet was nine and ten and Rosalind was seven and eight that they discovered each other, how much they needed each other, and how much they had to offer each other as sisters. Their hairstyles made them loners—making Rosalind more shy than ever and Linnet more nervous and socially clumsy, so they were forced to depend on each other for company most of the time. Through this Rosalind discovered that she needed her sister's size, strength, and maturity, for, oddly, Linnet had a tremendous "way with her" in dealing with younger children. She could, through her behavior, inspire a kind of confidence. And Linnet discovered that Rosalind could help her with her work. Rosalind would teach more patiently than even her tutors. She would read to Linnet, even do assignments for her, so that Linnet could be free to play with her. Yet all was far from rosy: each used the other's dependence in power plays. Linnet was often intolerably bossy and officious, while Rosalind became petty, disagreeably capricious, and argumentative. But it was undoubtedly the flowering of their sisterhood in these years that helped Linnet more than all the professional help or mainstreaming efforts we could scrape money together to buy.

One night, for instance, I saw Rosalind in my study, hard at work on one of Linnet's assignments. "You're not supposed to be doing Linnet's work," I said, somewhat irritated.

Rosalind looked up from her work with the supremely casual élan of preoccupied delight and unperturbed puzzlement that only a child in a certain mood can achieve: "Oh, this is something she could never learn anyway. That's why I'm doing it. Besides, she is my sister. If I don't cheat for her, who will?"

"I think we ought to cut out all this treatment stuff with Linnet," I told Ida one day. "I think it is a waste of time and money, and that she'll grow out of this L.D. thing as she gets older."

Ida looked at me fiercely. "Grow out of it? Is something wrong with you? We're not dealing with an allergy here or something like that. This child's future is at stake and, all of sudden, you want to be Mr. Casual. How the hell is she going to grow out of it?"

"As she gets older, she'll understand better what she can and cannot do. She'll also learn better to compensate for what she can't do. How to deceive people into thinking she knows something when she doesn't. We all do that.

Her problem is that she doesn't know how to do that yet, that she makes what she doesn't know obvious. She puts it right out there. Suddenly it's a problem for her teacher or her tutor or for us or for somebody. It's not a matter of what she needs to know. It's a matter of how well she can learn to mask what she doesn't know. It's not that Linnet doesn't know anything. She knows a great many things. She just doesn't know how to use what she knows."

"Well," Ida said slowly, "there might be something in what you say."

By the time the Afro period ended, the most serious stage of intervention with Linnet had ended as well. Not that she does not still have a tutor or that she has not been enrolled during the last few summers in a special school for learning-disabled children. But age has brought her greater confidence and greater skill at manipulating her knowledge. She has learned better how to accommodate, to dissimulate, to compensate.

A year ago, when she was twelve, she came home from school, straightened hair blowing stiffly in the wind, flushed with a richly earned sense of exquisite victory. She handed me her first report card that had no Cs, Ds, or unsatisfactories.

"I can't believe it, Daddy." she cried. "I made the Honor Roll. Can you believe it? I made the Honor Roll."

I grinned. "Let's celebrate. Let's make a dinner together."

While we bustled around the kitchen, whipping up, by bits and pieces, and through sheer ineptitude, a spaghetti dinner, Linnet turned to me and asked quietly:

"Do you think I am pretty, Daddy?"

"Sure," I said, trying to find the colander. "Prettiest kid I know."

"No," she said, "I mean seriously. The kids at school think I have a big nose and big feet. I think I'm just plain. I guess it's the L.D. that makes me ugly." And for a moment, all the joy of the good report card seemed drained away. I'm just a dumb, ugly black girl no matter what, she seemed to think, despite the straightened hair, the middle-class home with a room all her own, the creature comforts, a father's study lined with books to which she had free access.

"It isn't race," Ida once said to me.

"In America, it's always race," I said. "Even when it isn't or isn't supposed to be. It always is, even when it ain't."

"I never liked going to the Resource Room," Linnet told me a few months ago. "It's only mostly black kids who go there. So, all the white kids think that I'm just another dumb black kid. I didn't like that. That's why I worked so hard to get out of there. When they told me that I didn't have go to the Resource Room anymore except to take tests, man, that was the greatest thing that ever happened to me. Now I'm not seen anymore as just another dumb black kid. I'm like everybody else."

In 1916, E. Azalia Hackley, the Voice Teacher of the Race, as she was called in the black press, had published a book entitled *The Colored Girl Beautiful*. It was an odd little volume filled with advice for the black woman ranging from correcting the thick lips and "leaking" mouth and the wide Afric nose ("Grinning widens the nose and prevents its upward building, so grinning must cease") to telling married women that they must have children ("A woman who marries and does not intend to have children is merely an object of convenience who has sold herself"). It is, naturally, a book of its time, but at that moment in the kitchen with Linnet, how I wished that there was a flood of such books on the market, something particularly for black girls. What came to mind, specifically, was something Hackley wrote: "A little colored girl who wants to be pretty should be taught what 'pretty' really is."

I put down the steaming pot of noodles, grabbed Linnet by the shoulders, and stared straight into her face. Such a face it was too, as if I were, truly, looking at myself.

"You're a beautiful child, Linnet," I said. Then, smiling, taking her hand, and seeming to see, there, over her head, small angels nigger-ized to light, so thrilling that I could feel goose bumps all over, I said, "Why, you're beautiful enough to dance with, if I may." And taking her into my arms, helplessly charmed by the sheer elegance of our helplessness to the moment, around the kitchen we went, waltzing away.

Shortly after this I wrote a second poem for Linnet, in its way a commemoration of that evening.

The Cure
(FOR LINNET)

Touching the part in the middle of her hair,
It felt to him for all the world like an etching,
A severe tracing with a pencil, such as her face
    with tears
Was traced as he lifted it up: autotelic, he thought,
    as if unhappiness

Were, for him, after all, only an art form, like
    wearing one's hair:

Change your hairstyle and you're no longer
    unhappy, he thought childishly;

As she there, seated at her unfinished game of
    jacks, the small ball tumbled down,

Metal stars flung across the floor like so many
    awkward auroras.

And so he said, "Let's make spaghetti tonight
    together and eat in."

Moving around the kitchen, its worn floor, the
    father diced onions, found an old garlic,

The girl rinsed tomatoes, cut the green pepper,
    found spices in the back of a pantry.

She gathered the water in an old pot, and he tied
    an apron 'round his waist,

Covered the girl's hair with a kerchief so she
    looked, for all the world,

Like his sister, when, as a child, he watched her tie
    kerchiefs 'round her head.

And boyishly he told bad jokes like: "When is a
    door not a door?"

"When it's a jar, Daddy," the girl said impatiently,
    but smiling all the same.

It had not occurred to either the man or the girl
    that perhaps

This is the way praying is or that the answer to
    praying is, alas,

Prayer, a prayer for our praying to which we must
   listen
To know that the answer to our prayers is the act
   of praying
For an answer to them, not on our knees, but on
   the kitchen floor, worn as it is,
As the man and the girl, unknowingly, glided by
   each other, lightly,
In step, making the meal as a rhythm, together, a
   couple arrayed
With divine ordinariness as if it were, this kitchen,
   the starlight of a ballroom,
As if all magic were just the doing of what must be
   done by someone
And as if all unhappiness were absolved by thinking how we, such sociable saints,
Mustn't step upon each other's toes in the doing of
   our simple chores,
In knowledge that our dancing is the gracious sum
   of one and one, our sum of grace.
(Ah, stardust on the kitchen floor, as we, in that
   light, count the steps to reach our own height.)
And they, father and child, the last couple, in
   answer to their prayer, for that one evening's
Short but stately chorus, richly danced with grace-
   ful industry into a beam of eternity.

LIFE WITH FATHER (ROSALIND'S QUERIES OR LESSONS FOR LIVING)

There is a certain affrighted look that only,
In retrospect, I realized, a black city boy could
    wear,
Out in the snow, his hand held aloft, his fingers
Webbed with flakes, his battered sneakers wet,
    weary
From busting broncos, standing between the
    trolley tracks, his cowboy
Hat tilted, o burnished buckaroo, with a dare
    upon his lips
That only those who understood nothing in life
    but fear could bear,
Could, pressed and plucky against the cold,
    witness without wonder.

"Come on," he said, "we're goin' out west to sell
    these shopping bags."
And out across the stores we went, the scout and I,
    hawking our wares, braced
Tightly against the range wind by the fire that only
    fear and cold could spark.
"Bang! Bang! You're dead!" he'd laughed, pointing
    a deadly finger, smiling,
And I, slouched with homage, imagined us both
    magically watched by rodeo angels,

Ahorsed, the cowboy hat receding, the scout
    leading, a nuanced rider, across the prairies.

—Gerald Early, "Destry Rides
    Again" (For a childhood friend)

"Did you always want to be a writer, Daddy?
Even when you were little?"

"Yes, I think so. Even though I thought I
would wind up doing something else."

"But when did you first know? When was
the first time you wanted to be a writer?"

"Let's see. I think it must have been this real
cold New Year's Day. And my mother had
taken me to the Mummer's Parade because on
every New Year's Day in Philadelphia these
men would dress in costumes and march down
Broad Street, the main street of the city.

"We were standing on the corner of Broad
and South, where we always stood, with all the
other black folk. And every once in a while my
mother would take me inside one of the jazz
clubs on the corner there, to get warm for a bit,
and then we would go back out to watch some
more. I liked doing this very much.

"So, once when we go inside this club I see
that the musicians had set up their instruments
and I guess they were going to play a matinee
show or something, although as a boy at the

time I really wasn't aware of what exactly was going on or why those instruments were out there. And I remember that I was amazed by this tenor saxophone. It was so shiny, golden, and it seemed monstrously big. I thought the thing was made out of pure gold. I thought it was something Arabian, something straight out of a fairy tale. I thought that sax had to be worth a million dollars. And, let me tell you, it seemed like the coolest thing on earth. I just thought: 'Wow, I bet that's a cool thing to play or, better yet, just to walk around the street with that thing, shiny gold like that, coiled like a snake.' I just couldn't take my eyes off that thing. Even when my mother took me back outside, I kept straining to look through the club's big bay window to get another look at that sax."

"You wanted to play it, Daddy?"

"No, no, I didn't want to play it. For the first time, I felt an urge I had never felt before. I didn't want to play it. I wanted to describe it."

"You know, Daddy, when we were in that store the other day, I was looking at the candy and the clerk wasn't even paying attention to me and I thought, 'Boy, it would be easy just to take some stuff and put it in my pocket and nobody would know.' But I didn't because I knew it would be wrong and you and Mommy wouldn't like it."

"That was smart. Never steal! It's low. It's filthy. And just because the clerk isn't watching you doesn't mean that someone else who works for that store isn't. Besides, it makes white people think they have a power over you by making you stoop to stealing their merchandise. I would never let anybody think that they could possibly possess anything that would make me steal. My honor and self-worth are more to me than anything that anybody owns. You always buy and keep your dignity. If you cannot buy, then you do without."

"I know, Daddy, you've told me that before. I know the big race lesson and all that. But I kinda wanted to, for a second. You know, I was kinda tempted to steal something. It seemed so easy. But I knew it was wrong. Did you ever steal anything, Daddy, when you were a kid?"

"Yeah, sure I did. When I was around thirteen. But I learned a lesson when I was caught. I used to go to this bookstore in Philadelphia called Robbin's Books. And once, I wanted this book called *Sex and Racism in America* by Calvin Hernton."

"Hey, that sounds like pornography or something. Shame on you, Daddy. Buying pornography when you were thirteen. And then telling your daughter about it. What kind of a father are you anyway? I might have to call the child abuse hotline on this."

"The book wasn't pornography, Miss Wiseacre. It was a study of interracial sex. But for me at the time, I must admit, that was pretty heady stuff.

"I really wanted this book and I had enough money to buy it because I was working two jobs then. But it seemed so easy to just steal it. So that's what I did. Just slipped it into my pocket and walked out of the store and nothing happened. I said to myself, 'Boy, this stealing stuff is as easy as pie.' So, the next week I go back to the store and perhaps I am in the store for five or ten minutes, looking at titles, browsing, but not thinking about stealing anything because, oddly enough, stealing that book made me feel funny and I didn't want to do that again. All of a sudden this older white man comes up beside me and starts screaming at me, 'Get out of this store! Get out of here! Get out of here! We don't want thieves in here!' I was totally bewildered. I hadn't stolen anything. He started shoving me, literally shoving me, out of the store. He pushed me straight out of the door and onto the sidewalk, where I fell on the dirty ground at the feet of a bunch of passers-by. I was never so embarrassed in my life. The customers in the store had watched in surprise and disgust and amusement. The passers-by just walked over me or around me. I couldn't figure out what had happened to me. How did he know I had stolen a book before? At any rate, I ran all the way home. Must have been about twenty blocks, but I had to get out of there, away from my embarrassment and shame. I decided I'd rather die than steal anything.

"And do you know that I never went back in that store for years. I was too afraid and embarrassed. At least seven years went by before I went back in that store. By then I was a college student. I figured the guy who threw me out of the store couldn't possibly still be working there and even if he were he couldn't possibly remember me because it had been more than a half dozen years since that happened.

"So I selected a few books and was waiting in line to check out, and I see the guy at the register is the same elderly white guy who threw me out of the store when I was kid. But I'm not very concerned because I know he just couldn't possibly remember me.

"When he finally rings me out, he starts a little small talk. He asks me a few questions, finally getting around to the fact that I am a student.

"'Where do you go to school?'

"'Penn. I'm a sophomore.'

"'That's impressive. Good luck to you.'

"Then, right after paying for my purchases and as I'm about to leave the store, he said, 'I'm glad you put our books to such a good use when you were a boy.' And he winked. I couldn't believe it! All I could do was shrug and get out of that store. And that was my brief career as a thief."

"A future professor who steals books as a boy—what a concept! Would you give me a whipping if I ever stole something?"

"Yes, without a doubt. Even if you were thirty years old."

A Racial Education, Part One

"When did you join the colored race?" Sarah asked, sniggling.

"I never joined," Cross said.

—Richard Wright, *The Outsider*

...and that no people come into possession of a culture without having paid a heavy price for it.

—James Baldwin, "Equal in Paris"

There are rituals of a sort, verbal rituals, that I have with my daughters, conversations that keep getting repeated and that are never resolved because they were not meant to be—the sheer impenetrability of it, the mystery, provides the same comfort, after a bit, as religion—and the repetition, in its way, becomes the resolution.

"Why do you keep asking that, Daddy?" Linnet will ask. "You get the same answer all the time."

"Maybe just one time you will answer something different," I say.

"Well, if we were going to answer something different, you would know before you ask. Then, you wouldn't have to ask the question."

"What did you just say?" I ask, feigning

astonishment. "I think you may have bordered on something profound."

"Very funny," Linnet cracks. "You certainly didn't."

Periodically—let's say, about every three or four months—I will have a conversation with my daughters that begins something like this:

"Don't you guys think you ought to get to know a few more black kids at school?" I will ask, glancing from whatever it is I am reading, and shooting the question, like a darting non sequitur, out of nowhere, unconnected with whatever it was we may have been discussing, or causing a sudden rupture in the long period of silence that preceded it.

The response to this is the sort of genial if exaggerated exasperation that parents are likely to elicit from their children when they ask what can only be understood by their children's impatient and unforgiving minds as an officious, nay, a stupid question. Linnet and Rosalind stand poised, trying to fend off the possibility of a lecture with the good grace of taking me, or at least the question, somewhat seriously.

"No," Rosalind or Linnet will say, "we don't think we ought to have a few more black friends. We have as many as we want, thank you very much."

"But, from what I can tell," I rejoin, "you have no black friends at all. None come to the house. None call you up. I just thought it might be good not to have a social life that is 'too white.'"

"There he goes with the race thing again," Linnet or Rosalind will reply. "Why is it so important that we have to have black friends? Is it because we're black? You have to have more in common than just being black, you know."

And so the conversation, at this point, comes to a halt; my daughters having scored a quality point, as it were. I cannot take the questions posed by Linnet and Rosalind lightly or answer them glibly. Yet for me to form persuasive answers is not so easily achieved. Linnet and Rosalind live in a white, middle-class world, a comfortable life that might, to some, appear to be a decidedly mixed destiny, philistine and conformist as it can be, but that, in truth, must be acknowledged as, if not the best of all possible lives, certainly the best of the good many other lives that, realistically, my daughters could be living.

They attend a predominantly white (though decidedly not all-white) school. ("The place seems to be crawling with black kids to me," Linnet says. "It's only your racial imagination," I say, laughing. "You haven't lived among black kids until you revisit some of the haunts I was educated in.") They live in an almost all-white neighborhood. Ida and I work at a major, white university and socialize, in large measure, with many of the whites we have come to know through our jobs and through Ida's association with the Junior League and her board-of-trustees memberships in several social-service agencies.

Ida and I are the beneficiaries (inadvertent in the sense that we never quite sought *it* and intentional in the sense that *it* was certainly sought for us) of Martin Luther King, Jr.'s dream of an integrated America—indeed, beneficiaries of the sacrifices made by the many, black and white, during the civil-rights years in America, from 1955 through 1965, when we both were children. We live a thoroughly integrated life that would have been impossible for either our grandparents or our parents. (Although I must admit that my mother—a high school dropout at sixteen and a widow at twenty-three—reared me and my two sisters in an Italian working-class neighborhood with no problem. "That wouldn't have happened," a black woman academic said to me once, "if your mother was not a widow. If your father was still alive, the neighborhood would have responded differently to the presence of a black man." "I guess you're right about that," I said, "but my mother told me that my father felt that the people who most wounded him, most tortured him, most abused him in his life were Negroes. I was told once that he thought one of the nice things about dying was that he would be 'free from having to be around niggers.' Now, we can talk about the self-hatred of the oppressed, but what my father did not like about black folk was that they would not let him have his own opinions, see the world the way he wanted to see it. He felt he was being crushed by their brutal and mindless urge for conformity in an atmosphere of never-ending complaint. I am, naturally, very sympathetic to that. Maybe he would have wound up hating the Italians as well, but I am not as sure of that as you are.") Ida and I are both sufficiently grateful for the pain endured on our behalf. We feel sufficiently unworthy of our bounty, and are sufficiently bemused by our fate, to qualify as being as blandly and anxiously bourgeois as our white neighbors.

There is something oddly daunting about this black, middle-class life. At cocktail parties, one is never sure if one's white neighbors are smiling at you with the self-satisfaction of knowing, with you before them as living and incontrovertible proof, that the American Dream works for everyone, or with the faint contempt that their accomplishments cannot be much if Negroes, without benefit of middle-class parents, can do in ten or twenty years of Affirmative Action what the systematic privilege of racism, hard work, and luck took the whites a few generations to get. Or perhaps they think it is *solely* because of Affirmative Action that you can have, though a great deal more precariously in most cases, what they have. There are moments, every now and again, in your relationship with your white neighbors when this creeps into your mind and you feel that they think you to be both more and less than human in one fell swoop.

And you smile, too, at the thought of being something of a novelty, being interesting to and accepted by a group of people largely because they are convinced of a contradiction: that while you seem very familiar and similar, at the core you are something strikingly, remarkably different. (A certain minor, off-key tension can exist between middle-class blacks and whites, subtle but sure, even though they like each other deeply and well.) In this age of multiculturalism, it pays to be different, something non-

European is good, and something victimized by Europeans is even better; although, paraphrasing Edgar Allan Poe, the old adage must be kept in mind: be different, be different, but not too different! You smile because, after all, you are a great deal more comfortable with whites than they generally are with you because you have had to succeed in their world and on their terms, so you are used to interacting with them. You smile, finally, because you think your middle-class success, such as it is, could have been achieved by your great-grandparents or at least your grandparents and probably should have been. You do not think you have risen very rapidly from your working-class origins, from your domestic origins, remembering, as Ida and I can, that many of our relatives cleaned white people's homes. Ida and I have said more than once to each other that all of this bourgeois cornucopia seems a few generations overdue. "The good life is not all that good," Ida once intoned, "and a lot more black folk should have had it a hell of lot of earlier, if working hard was supposed to get it for you."

"If you want us to have black friends, why don't you move to a black neighborhood and have us go to a black school?" Linnet once asked me, a kind of parting shot, if you will.

For, from the child's tactical viewpoint, the thought is: "If the parent wishes me to do something, and I cannot or will not do it, then I must devise a way to blame the parent for failing to make the parent happy."

So this, too, is a fair question. If it is so important to us that she and her sister should have black friends, why have we put them in an environment where they are likely to be thwarted in any expectation to please their parents in that regard? And how important, truly, can it be to us if we live in such a neighborhood and socialize with other African Americans occasionally but not so frequently as we used to because it takes such a concerted effort now?

❖

"I had a teacher once named Mr. King," I tell Linnet and Rosalind one afternoon. "He taught me in the fourth and fifth grades, but I knew him, interacted with him, until I was young adult. I would go back to my elementary school often just to talk to him. He always had time to hear what I had to say. He gave me a copy of a book called *Portrait of the Artist as a Young Man* when I was about fourteen, I think. The book made a big impression on me.

"One day, when I was about fifteen or so, I decided that I wanted to study karate at the YMCA because bigger boys were always beating me up. But I needed to buy a *gi* to take the lessons and a *gi* cost thirty dollars. And thirty dollars was a lot of money for a kid back in the mid-1960s. I didn't have much money because, during that span of time when I was most interested in this, about seven months, I was not working. I was taking what you might call a sabbatical. I had been working steadily since I was about nine and I wanted some time away from scuffling for pennies. I didn't want to ask my mother for the money, so I asked Mr. King."

"Did he give it to you?" Rosalind asked.

"Yes. I mean, I sold him my books. I just couldn't ask him outright for the money. So I sold him the only things I possessed that were worth anything to me. My books. I had, maybe, thirty paperbacks. James Baldwin, Thomas Wolfe, Aldous Huxley, George Orwell, J. D. Salinger, Edgar Rice Burroughs, all my favorite authors at the time. I sold him the books for fifteen dollars."

"Wow, you didn't sell them for much," Linnet said.

"Books weren't so expensive then. Besides, I had half the amount of money I needed, money I had saved from working," I said.

"Well, what would he want with your old paperbacks anyway."

"At the time, I didn't think about that. I just knew I was giving up something important. But I had to have the karate lessons and so I had to have the *gi*. But do you know what he did?"

"He either gave the books back to you or he never took them," Linnet ventured.

I was a bit disappointed at having my thunder stolen.

"Well, yeah, that's right. He never took the books."

"Figures," said Linnet. "Otherwise, why the heck would you be telling us the story? Another wonderful tale about growing up black and living in the city."

"A suburban life nowadays, whether black or white, but especially for blacks where it can be very fragmenting," I said. "I don't think it lends itself to such a sense of neighborhood, of people being together. Maybe it's because we're black. I don't know. I wish you guys didn't love it so much."

"Move us somewhere else," Rosalind said. "We can't stop you. But don't blame us that you're living here."

❖

Linnet and Rosalind have been to Philadelphia only once to see my family. Rosalind was five and Linnet was seven, and they cried and begged me to take them back to St. Louis. It was during the time I was at the University of Kansas, and it was Ida's suggestion that I take them to Philadelphia. She thought it would be a good idea for some sort of father-daughter bonding, or perhaps she wanted to have the children away for a week. I am not really sure why I took them—certainly not from a sense of closeness to my family, because to many there I am a stranger, an alien—but I supposed I wanted my family to see them, and all my relatives were interested in seeing "Jerry's children." Linnet and Rosalind were shocked that I was related to people who were, many of them—though by no means all of them—poor or working-class, who seemed loud and crude, who lived in tiny houses in run-down neighborhoods. Unwed mothers, people who spoke the word *nigger*, who liked to jive around, who exaggerated and lied freely and whose conversation, often boisterous and melodramatic, was not always to be taken seriously.

But it was here that I grew up.

"Who is so-and-so's father?" Linnet asked me.

"I don't know who her father is," I said.

"Oh, does he work a job that takes him far away?" Linnet pressed.

"I don't know. But her father does not live with her and her mother."

"Oh, are they divorced?" Linnet continued.

"No, the father and so-and-so's mother were never married," I said.

"Oh, but I thought you couldn't have babies if you weren't married," she said, completely puzzled.

"Why do your cousins have such funny names?" Rosalind asked.

"Their names are not funny. They have African names," I said.

"Are they Africans?" Rosalind asked.

"No, their parents just wanted to give them African names," I said.

"Why didn't you give us African names?" Rosalind pressed.

"Because my father and mother didn't have one, and neither do I," I said, grinning.

"I cannot deny my relatives," I told Linnet and Rosalind privately, during a tense moment when they ran away from my Uncle George, deeply frightened by his raucous laughter. "They are my blood."

"I still don't like them," they cried.

"I'm not asking you to like them. But I wish

you would be less afraid and more open to them. Nobody's going to hurt you. They're excited to see you."

But even in my exhortations to my children to reach, I stood guard over them, overprotective and wary, as if I thought my relatives might wound them, might injure them in a clumsy, "niggerish" way. Perhaps my children's awkwardness and unhappiness with this situation merely mirrored my own.

"Jerry," my mother told me during the visit, "you had better expose these kids more to black folk and get 'em out of the suburbs."

"They'll be all right, Mom," I said. "This is all pretty new to them. Besides, they've never seen most of these people before. About the suburbs: I can't pretend to be something I no longer am, or perhaps I never was. I can't go back. Inner-city Philadelphia is a long way away from me now."

It was only my oldest sister's daughters, Hathor and Aminta, that made this trip in any way tolerable for Linnet and Rosalind. Discovering Hathor, a Down's syndrome child, was particularly gratifying to Linnet, who became convinced through this that she herself was not retarded, although at this time she was struggling mightily in school.

We spent one day with them touring some historic spots in the city and ending at the Please Touch Museum, a place especially built for children's inquiry and play. We go back to my mother's house by elevated train, the first time Linnet and Rosalind have traveled that way, and they are excited by the crowd, the noise, the rush, buoyant, by turns, wide-eyed and atwitter like children, then giggling and secretive like little girls.

"Will Hathor always have to live with her mother?" Linnet asked that evening.

"Maybe," I said. "Sometimes, Down's syndrome adults can live on their own, mostly in supervised situations with others like themselves."

"But when I grow up I can live on my own, can't I?"

"Sure you can. What makes you think you couldn't?"

But my "black" life frightened my daughters, who thought it a foreign culture, another country. "I don't remember being poor when I grew up," I told them. "It's not the comforts that make life bearable. It's the life that makes the comforts dispensable." This seemed a good lesson at the time, and it was, in its way, true or at least not such a huge untruth as to compromise me by saying it. Several years later when we are discussing the possibility of making another trip to Philadelphia, Linnet says, blandly:

"I guess you don't like your family much and they don't like you much. You don't see them very often and they don't come to see you."

"It's probably best that way," I say at last.

A RACIAL EDUCATION, PART TWO

"The black kids at school are stupid," Rosalind said angrily as she slammed the door coming home from school one day.

"How so?" I asked, curious about this outburst.

"Do you know what they said to me today? They said I must be biracial, that one of my parents must be white," she said, totally confounded.

"Why do they believe that?" I inquired.

"Because of the way I talk. They say I sound like a white person, so one of my parents must be white. They're so stupid. What am I supposed to do? Talk like them? Go around cursing all the time or saying 'y'all' and 'ain't' and stuff like that? Is that supposed to be the way black people talk? I know you and Mommy and your black friends, and the black people at church, and none of you guys talk like that. What am I supposed to sound like, a rap record? I don't like being called white. I'm not white and I'm not biracial. I think they're just ignorant."

I tried to explain to Rosalind that both I and my sisters, when we were children, were often told the same thing. I suggested that perhaps she was overreacting, taking the kids' remarks too seriously. Although, as I remember the remarks of the children when I was little, I thought it strange because the persons I most wanted to sound like were Sidney Poitier (after each time I saw a Sidney Poitier movie I would try to imitate how he walked, how he held his hands, the inflections of his voice) and my grade school teacher, Mr. Lloyd R. King, and I doubt if my sisters had anyone white in mind either: "Jerry and them sound just like white people, all educated and everything," the black kids of the neighborhood would say.

"When black kids told me that when I was young, it was a kind of perverse, left-handed compliment," I said to Rosalind. "They thought you were educated, that you were smart. It's a shame they associate being educated with being white, but that's the way it was and, I guess, still is. But you should try to reach out to them more. I'm sure they didn't mean to insult you when they told you that."

This led Rosalind to a sort of general criticism. "Some of the black kids are okay. But some, especially the boys, act crazy. They're always acting up in class, in the lunchroom, always going to see the principal."

"But you must remember," I replied to Rosalind, "a lot of these kids have severe problems, and for many, busing isn't an easy experience. Besides, not everyone has had your advantages." (This does not seem, in retrospect, so *foolish* a thing to say to a child as it seems a terribly over-measured *adult* thing to say. In the end, Necile the nymph is right when she tells Santa Claus in L. Frank Baum's *The Life and Adventures of Santa Claus:* "Riches are like a gown which may be put on or taken away, leaving the child unchanged." Nothing touches a child so much as the other humans of which it partakes and with whom it bonds. And so what I said to Rosalind shows how far removed we parents can be from what our children understand.)

Both my wife and I have tried, a bit half-heartedly I must admit, a number of ventures to help our children "relate to their blackness," so to speak, because the problem with black friends grows, I would guess, from how my children understand what being black is. There is a certain contradictory frenzy, a conflicted sloth, to all of this.

"I'm tired of all this race stuff," Ida said to me once, exasperated by it all. "Why do black people always have to carry around a race burden? I want my children to be able to eat, go to the bathroom, and sleep, live their lives without always having to think that a Negro is doing it or to care what other black folk are doing."

"Maybe your survival depends upon your race consciousness," I ventured.

"My survival doesn't depend on any such damn thing," Ida snapped back. "And neither does my sanity. But there are a lot of herd-instinct, cowardly, crab-in-a-basket Negroes and some do-good liberal whites who want you to think that."

But it was Ida who led the way with her membership in Jack and Jill, a black organization, run by mothers, whose sole purpose is to get together black, middle-class children who are estranged from each other because, alas, of integration. My wife was particularly up for this at one time because she was a bit chary about the possibility that our daughters might date white boys when they reached dating age.

Linnet, in recent years, has been coming home talking about how much she likes white movie stars like Christian Bale and Christian Slater, and she even had a crush on a white school-mate for a time.

"What's the big deal?" Rosalind said to me once. "There are two black girls at school who date white boys. Who cares?"

"Well, I guess this is a new day and age," I said, laughing.

"Yeah, Daddy, get with the program. You still think the covers of those Mandingo books are hot stuff."

"My daughter, the comedian," I quipped. "Who writes your material? Or are you actu-ally responsible for it all on your own?"

It is, indeed, the prospect of interracial dating that, for the most part, brings the women of Jack and Jill together. Although I am less concerned about interracial dating than some other black parents I know, not because I do not think it is a possibility for my children but because I am more inclined to let them find happiness wherever they can, I cannot say that I am entirely at ease with it. What I object to in "interracial relationships" is some black person's being con-vinced that he or she cannot possibly date another black person because there is none who is worthy—indeed, being drawn to whites simply for snobbish or status reasons. This seems to me to be just another expression of internalized inferiority. I do not mind if my daughters marry whites, but I would feel deeply distressed if I felt this had happened because they thought whites to be superior to the blacks they knew. Perhaps this is why their having black friends is important—nay, essential, according to Ida's thinking for a time—to their well-being. She firmly believed, as she told me, that black Americans cannot face whites as equals, comfortable in a common culture and sharing a common set of terms and values, if they feel that their own group has nothing to offer, provides no sense of who or what they are. But she didn't believe that very deeply or for very long, in fact.

My wife's venture with Jack and Jill did not work out well for two reasons: First, she thought it was an imposition that only women were allowed to participate in the organization. "We need couples in this, so the burden does not have to be only on one parent. Most of these black women in the group work, just like me, so why the heck do they run an organization as if they were middle-class white women sitting at home?"

Second, Rosalind and Linnet did not like

"the events" they attended, or at least, did not like the company they were forced to keep. The kids "were worse than the black kids at school," Linnet said. "These kids aren't bad, they're bratty. Besides, all of this is so fake, so false. What do we have in common except we're black yuppie kids?"

"That should be enough," I said.

"Well, it isn't," Linnet said with finality. "Are you friends with people just because they're professors?" Contrived? Linnet was right. It was, although whites often bring their children together purely for such social purposes. This was something my daughters did not or could not understand and appreciate. In any case, they did not profit from it the way some of the other children did.

Naturally, as a college professor who runs a black-studies program, my house is filled to the rafters with books by and about black people. I probably own more such books than virtually anyone else in St. Louis. I am not Afrocentric. I do not celebrate "African" ceremonies, so African American culture is not "demonstrated" in my house. But hardly a week goes by when I do not engage Ida in serious discussion about some aspect of African American culture or politics. Yet there is, with rare exception, something dispassionate, detached, something that seems curiously without the intensity of identification. My children are awash in exposure to African American culture. They know what the Harlem Renaissance is, who Countee Cullen was, who Miles Davis and Thelonious Monk were. But this has little emotional impact on them—perhaps because there is little emotional impact of any of this knowledge on me. I have taken them, on several occasions, to Afrocentric bookstores, or allowed them to order anything they wish from Afrocentric catalogues.

"Do I have to buy something, Daddy?" Rosalind asks. "I will if it makes you happy. But I really don't want anything."

"Why? I understand the black kids at school wear Malcolm X shirts and stuff like that. I thought you might want something like that, too."

"No, I don't like that stuff that the black kids wear," Linnet says. "They're these Africa-crazy kids and they hate me. They go around wearing these Mother Africa shirts and stuff like that. They call me and Ros Oreos and everything. But in history class they couldn't even name any countries in Africa when the teacher asked. I was naming bunches and bunches of countries from the stuff I read here at home. But they didn't know anything, yet they want to think they're so black. I don't want anything to do with them or wear anything they wear. I'm black and I'm not ashamed of it. And I don't need a shirt to tell anybody I'm black or to tell anybody I'm not ashamed. All I have to do is live my life the way *I* want to."

And in a way I was relieved to hear her say this: the commodification of African American politics and culture, through the low-brow and middle-brow impulses of Afrocentrism, strikes me not as a solution to the problem of black identity, but simply a capitulation to the larger problem of what it means to be an American. For many Americans, it means precisely what one can buy and consume, and an identity, political or otherwise, becomes just another sign of status, a billboard of falsely conceived pride mixed with a hotly induced resentment, not the hard-fought realization of the complexities of consciousness.

"You could just play along with them," I said.

"I don't want to play along with people who don't want to accept me for what I am," Linnet said sharply.

❖

One night, we sat in a circle on the floor and I read to them Etheridge Knight's famous poem, "The Idea of Ancestry." They were silent for a while after hearing it. Then they wanted to know if Etheridge Knight was really in prison when he wrote the poem and if he was really a drug addict.

Suddenly, Rosalind blurted out: "I don't like that poem. Are you trying to tell us something about being black, Daddy? Well, I don't care. I don't like that poem." Then she rose and left the room. I turned to Linnet.

"What did you think?" I asked.

"I liked it," Linnet said. "I thought it was a nice poem. Are you mad Ros didn't like it?"

"No," I said, "not at all. She is entitled to like or dislike whatever she chooses."

"Will you ask her why she didn't like it?"

"No," I said thoughtfully. "She has her reasons. Let's leave it at that."

Just as suddenly Rosalind reentered the room, carrying a book: "Read this," she said, then as an afterthought, shyly, "if you don't mind." It was a copy of some children's poems by Robert Louis Stevenson.

I took the book, Rosalind retook her place on the floor, and I began to read.

Why is 'blackness' on issue? Because it is that which had nurtured you...

PART II

GRACELAND:
WHAT WE HOPE TO BE

*But the doings of their elders, unless where they
are speakingly picturesque or recommend themselves by the quality of being easily imitable, they
let them go over their heads (as we say) without
the least regard. If it were not for this perpetual
imitation, we should be tempted to fancy they
despised us outright, or only considered us in the
light of creatures brutally strong and brutally silly;
among whom they condescended to dwell in obe-
dience like a philosopher at a barbarous court.*

> —Robert Louis Stevenson,
> "Child's Play"

*It comes back again to you:
Not the blank insistent wave,
The broken vanity of the burnt-over beach,
The high-pitched mongrel cry of gulls
Like the lyricism of loneliness, cracked echo.*

*The immensity returns, the wasteful glory
That overruns and overwhelms the eye,*

God's boyish scrim, a magical show,
All light and more light, silken and stark,
All stair and star, all space and sand,
Like some miracle, breaking and spiraling,
Like some grand toys strewn about the void,
Like girlish laughter filling a morning,
Dim-voiced verses bunched and splintered,
As two children run along the shore
Chasing a boyish God, a promised horizon, the
*   tender*
Hope and mercy of a perfectly tempered tomorrow.

—Gerald Early, "With Linnet and
Rosalind at the Pacific Ocean"

Rosalind's diary, verbatim

November 1, 1992 (continued)

Well anyway on to my family. Well there are 5 of us. My mom (Ida Early) my dad (Gerald Early) my sister (Linnet Early) and the dog (Einstein Early) and me. We live on 9 Harvest Street and our telephone # is 569-1990. My mom is really nice, kind of pesky and very silly. My dad is a person who likes to be alone and is always wrapped up in his work. But when he isn't wrapped up in his work he's funny and very fun to be around. My sister is pesky and bratty. She's also very MEAN!!! In other words, she's okay. Our dog is a Golden Retriever he is very nice kind and doesn't speak (bark). Oh and it's a male around 6 or 7 [years old] we got him last year on December 30th to be exact.

Now about me I'm 10 I go to Steger I have lots of friends and I'm a plain sugar-holic. I love any kinds of sweets except coconuts, nuts, and dark chocolate ew, ew, ew. Well I also like to play dolls but I keep that a secret or else there goes my reputation (Oh and I also forget something about my dad he got sugery [surgery] and is kind of mean.)

Midwestern Snow

It came at the end of January and was the worst snowstorm of the dozen years Ida and I had been in St. Louis, even more severe than the one we encountered when we first moved to St. Louis in 1982. That first storm paralyzed the city for days, but it hardly disturbed us in our poverty. (We had, as St. Louisan Chuck Berry once sang, no particular place to go, and I could, in those days, walk to the university. Ida was unemployed.) Besides, as we smugly told ourselves, we were accustomed to that sort of thing, having just lived in Ithaca, New York for several years. We had just arrived from Ithaca on New Year's Day, with a battered, rusted-out Vega, piled high with household goods, diapers, baby bottles, suitcases, and the like. For most of the ride Linnet sat quietly in the back in her car seat, almost Zenlike in her indifference to her obvious discomfort, while her newborn sister, Rosalind, cried most of the journey.

"I thought this was the South. Now, we're getting those Laura Ingalls Wilder/Willa Cather snowstorms." I said to Ida when I saw that first snow in 1982.

Ida reminded me that it was the Midwest, *not* the South.

"Oh," I moaned, "the godforsaken American Midwest. I thought Missouri was south. They had slavery here, didn't they? How the heck did we wind up here?"

"You needed a job in order to pay Rosalind's delivery bill and this was the only one that started in January instead of next September. Besides, at one point in America, slavery was everywhere."

That first mammoth snowstorm only intensified my dislike of St. Louis and the Midwest, a strange, unpalatable place for an easterner like myself. I imagined that we would stay only for a year or two.

"Good gracious, it's like another country out here," I told Ida.

"Your education has been temporarily interrupted by Mother Nature," I trumpeted to Linnet and Rosalind, darting from one room to the other, almost as excited as a kid myself. "Your wish came true. There's a ton of snow outside. The third worst storm in St. Louis since the National Weather Service started keeping records, the news says. So, have fun."

"Really? Let me see." Linnet ran to the window, her bare feet gently smacking the floor.

"Wow, what a lot of snow! And no school, too!"

I began the arduous work of shoveling out our driveway, envious of the neighbor down the street whose whirring snow remover effortlessly shot the snow in white arcs into the street. Although Linnet and Rosalind had a day off, the university was open and I needed to get there to finish up some work.

"Need some help?" I turned and Rosalind was behind me, bundled like a space visitor: huge boots, huge gloves, huge parka, a scarf that veiled her face. She looked hilarious, a cross between a football player and the Mummy. I thought of a chant that I had heard on a record: "Sun-Ra and His Band from Outer Space Will Entertain You Now." She's decked out well enough to audition for the Myth-Science Arkestra, I thought. I had been at work for perhaps forty or so minutes. I was pouring sweat, my arms felt tired, and my bent back was killing me. The last time it had snowed Ida had shoveled the driveway by herself.

"What's the matter?" she crowed from a window. "Male pride got you? Can't have the little wifey show you up?"

"I've got to get to work. Besides, you aren't all that little," I yelled.

I smiled at Rosalind for a moment, enjoying the sensation of straightening my back. The snow glared in the sun and hurt my eyes.

"No, Rosalind, go ahead and play. I'll take care of this."

"You don't like help, do you, Daddy?" Rosalind asked.

"I don't need it here. Go play and enjoy yourself."

But what she said reminded me of the Thanksgiving of my twelfth year. I had just signed on for a paper route, delivering the Philadelphia *Inquirer.* The manager drove me around the route the day before and it looked easy enough: forty-three daily papers that I had to deliver before 7:15 A.M., so I would have time to clean up, eat breakfast, and make it to school by 8:45. He told me the papers would usually be delivered to me by 5:30 but that since tomorrow was a holiday, they would be there even earlier and I would have more time to deliver them as I didn't have to go to school. What he didn't tell me was that the Thanksgiving edition of the paper was the biggest of the year, larger even than a normal Sunday paper. A friend was going to lend me a shopping cart to deliver the Sundays but I didn't figure I would need one for the weeklies. I was more than a bit chagrined when I came out to find stacks and stacks of papers, what looked like hundreds, until I realized that it was only forty-four (one extra) very thick ones. The delivery bag I was given was strong enough to carry only three or four at a time. I tried very hard to think of a way to deliver them but realized that I had no alternative but to laboriously carry them, three or four at a time, until I had finished the route. It was a warm Thanksgiving, and after an hour I was pouring sweat, my shirt and jacket were drenched. The sun was up. It was a glowing morning. It felt as if I were walking the blocks of my neighborhoods hundreds of times. It took hours to deliver the papers. After a time, my mother came out. She watched me for a while, looking imperative yet comforting in that early autumn sun, then asked if I needed some help.

"It's not your route and it's not your responsibility," I said, doggedly stuffing papers in the sack, doggedly determined to finish the route no matter how long it took or how much my shoulder ached. "I don't want any help."

I know that that was actually what she wanted me to say. She went back in the house and made me a nice breakfast, something my mother rarely did for me once I had become that old. It was her way of saying how much she appreciated an act of such independence.

"Want to go for a ride with me down to campus?" I asked Rosalind when the driveway was finished, hours later.

"What do you want me for?" she asked.

"Company and ballast," I said.

"Which car are you taking?"

"Your mother's. It has better tires."

"As long as it's not that beat-up car of yours."

Even Rosalind was surprised by how slowly I had to drive, by how much snow clogged the roads. Streets that were normally two lanes were sometimes barely one. The landscape looked unfamiliar, like another planet, another country. A Sun-Ra song title kept buzzing through my head, "Other Planes of There." I could even hear John Gilmore and Marshall Allen screaming on their reeds, Ra on that ghostly, poorly tuned, poorly recorded piano. It somehow seemed appropriate, even calming in its turbulence, like a soundtrack for the gorgeous ghostliness of the snow, the unrelenting sun, the sharp, crackling outline of images on an automatic earth.

Then, out of nowhere, I heard myself say to Rosalind, "There are not many crimes committed in weather like this." I found myself in a mood—partly didactic, partly exhibitionist—

to tell a story. I did not know why I wanted to tell this story to Rosalind. I haven't any idea what I wanted her to learn from it. Perhaps I wanted her to think her father was something of a tough guy, someone who knew his way around or someone who could handle dire situations and dangerous circumstances, much like driving a car in a deep snow.

"I guess not. Even the criminals can't get out of their homes."

"Many years ago, when I worked for the municipal court system in Philadelphia and I interviewed incarcerated people to see if they might qualify to be released from jail without having to pay bail, I would enjoy days of bad weather, days like this, or days of very heavy rain. Few people were arrested. It was an easy time to work."

Rosalind did not understand what bail was, so I explained it, as well as the entire arraignment process.

"When I did this work, most people were in jail because they couldn't pay their bail, not because of any crime of which they had been convicted."

"Really?" said Rosalind, fascinated that crime and punishment seemed far more complex than the accounts given in the newspaper or on television shows. "Jail is full of innocent people?"

"No, not innocent. Most of them are not innocent. Let's just say poor and unlucky people, or just brutal people sometimes."

"Did you like that job, Daddy?"

"Well," I considered, for a moment, "there were a bunch of characters who got arrested. Transvestites who were male prostitutes who were always trying to find customers in the men's room at pornographic gay movie houses, women prostitutes who were all junkies and who all looked so bad that I wondered how they could find customers, lots of drug addicts with pus-swollen sores on the backs of their hands, one who threw up on my desk because he needed a fix."

"Wow, he must have really been sick."

"No, Ros, that was his way of telling me what he thought of the interview I was trying to conduct.

"There were number runners, tough guys. I was punched twice while working there. Cursed out, called everything but a child of God. Thieves of all sorts. Rapists, drunk drivers. It stank down there to high heaven and the people would do anything to get a cigarette. And everybody lied. Once, a prostitute down there even kissed me."

"Don't tell mommy that. She'll be jealous."

The woman, a down-and-out white prostitute with a bad drug habit, out of the blue, kissed me and I was so shocked, so repulsed by the act, that I fell over backward in my chair, trying to get away from the woman. "You're so cute and boyish," she said, grinning at me lewdly. "I'll bet you never had a girl and I bet you got a big fat dick, too." She winked. Scott Landau, the shift supervisor, and my fellow interviewers thought this was amusing, downright sidesplitting. "You've got yourself a girlfriend, Gerald." I must have washed my face six or seven times during the shift, trying to erase the memory of that kiss. That's the most foul thing anybody's ever done to me, I thought at the time. Another time, a man, a large man with a tough demeanor, and a nasty scar on his neck, was being interviewed and I asked him not to smoke. The space where we did the work was small, cramped, and smoking made it insufferable, ruining your clothes and hair with the odor.

He turned and said, "You asking me to stop smoking? After I been down this motherfucking hole for six hours and you, college boy, asking me to stop smoking?"

I told him that that was exactly what I was

asking him to do, and that he hadn't smoked so far, that a few more hours wouldn't kill him.

His eyes narrowed into red slits: "I'm gonna remember you, college boy, when I get outta here. I'm gonna definitely remember your ass. And I hope I see you somewhere on the street."

I returned his stare, never breaking eye contact. I should have been frightened by the mere thought of crossing this man. He had been arrested for murder six times in the last three years, all of his cases dismissed for "lack of witnesses." He was a well-known hit man for a crime syndicate in Philadelphia called the Black Mafia, an extortion, drug-peddling outfit that grew from some of the Nation of Islam mosques. Moreover, I knew how touchy most of the people were that I was forced to deal with, taking deadly umbrage at the slightest, most insignificant remark or gesture while, of course, accepting whole mountains of systematic abuse, straining at gnats to discharge the furious discomfort they had at the indigestion from swallowing camels. I was not afraid because I was convinced he was bluffing, just "selling woolf tickets," as folk used to say, to see if I would give in to him. Just some street manhood stuff.

If he sees me on the street, he won't do a thing to me. He didn't get where he is by hurting college boys. I'm as irrelevant to him as the air, I thought. I turned on my heels and walked away.

"Yeah, there were all kinds of characters," I continued. "A woman who kept getting arrested because she shot golf balls from her vagina in front of an audience."

"Wow," said Rosalind. "She could really do that? That's incredible!"

I said that I thought it was actually disgusting, that all of it was disgusting, that it was a carnival of filth. I said that when I left that job I felt not joy, but certainly a delightful sense of relief and release.

I don't know why I told Rosalind all of this. I didn't know what the point of the story was supposed to be. It was especially unusual because while I had, for the last few years, told them stories of my childhood, I almost never told them anything about my young adult life. In a way, I was beginning to wish that I had kept all this drivel to myself when a car jerked out from a side street in front of us and I swerved to avoid hitting it, skidding wildly down a hill. Rosalind was terrified. I could feel her fear. "Oh, my God!" she said. I grunted at the wheel, gripping it firmly but not too hard, letting my foot up from the brake, turning by increments to avoid the utility pole that we were bound to hit if we didn't stop skidding. Dammit, car, I thought, you will do my will. "Good Lord," I said aloud. Rosalind could only stare straight ahead. I glanced at her once. Please, God, I thought, don't let me kill this child. We narrowly missed the pole. The entire episode took, perhaps, ten seconds but it felt like ten hours. My shoulders ached from the tension.

We were silent for a moment.

"I thought we were going to die," she said.

"You're gonna die one day, Ros. But not today and not by my hand."

We decided to skip the trip to campus. I eased the car from the snowbank where it had landed, turned around, and started home.

"Daddy," Rosalind started out tentatively, "have you ever known a kid who died? I mean a kid you knew who died when you were a kid?"

I told her that I had and how it happened. A girl named Jacqueline, whom I knew in the fourth grade, died in a house fire caused by a space heater left on too long or something. One of those deaths one always reads about in the papers that happen during the winter to poor families.

"Well, didn't you feel sad about it? Did you cry when you learned about it?"

I told her I was mostly shocked because I didn't think kids could die. I didn't think anybody I knew could die. But other deaths happened, so I found out differently. When I thought about it, a fair number of kids I knew died well before adulthood.

When we arrived home and Rosalind opened the car door to get out, she said, slowly, "I thought I was going to die today."

"Well, I'm sorry. It's a little tricky driving in the snow. But everything turned out okay," I said, trying to lighten things a little.

"No, everything didn't turn out okay. You could have killed me. I'm never going to go driving with you in the snow again," she said angrily, and slammed the car door, startling me so that I jumped slightly. She walked, space-creature-like in her snowsuit, away. I felt disappointed in myself and frightened, not so much by the fact that I had nearly killed my daughter, as that she *realized* that I had nearly killed her. There was a certain horror in thinking about one's child's thinking about her own death as a real possibility. I surely was not the father I wanted to be, the father I imagined myself to be, who could handle difficult situations or who seemed completely in control. I felt bad, sitting in the car, in the cold, thinking that I had let Rosalind down, failed her. I was now afraid to think of what my daughter thought of me. I was beginning to get cold, sitting in the car, so I started walking toward the house, thinking that Ida would tell me that Rosalind would soon forget about the whole matter. And I was at least partly convinced that she would, but, although she never mentioned it again, I was never entirely sure that she had.

ROSALIND'S VERSION OF THE TRIP TO DISNEY WORLD (FROM ROSALIND'S DIARY, VERBATIM)

January 30, 1991

The most fun I probably ever had was when we traveled, my family was big on travel. Well my mom had a convention down in Orlando, Florida. That was back when I was seven. And we all got to go because they were having a special that all coach tickets cost $2.00. Well, soon we left. We were all going, my mom, Ida, my dad, Gerald, my sister, Linnet, and me, Rosalind. Our flight was connected. We were supposed to leave at 2:00 PM and then land in Atlanta, from there we would catch another flight and fly to Florida. We were going to be in Florida for three days!

Once we got to the airport it had begun to snow again, this was in the middle of January, we all had carry ons so no need to get the baggage checked. We went to our gate only to find that the flight had been delayed. We were all hungry so we got some food and ate at the airport. Then my sister and I went to go get lifesavers to prevent our ears from poping. Afterwards my sister (my sister was nine and I was seven so we didn't know any better) and I ran around the airport and we also got a ride in this car that always goes around the airport back to our gate. Then we waited and waited and waited. Finally we could leave.

We landed at 11:00 pm. When we got off the plane, lots of people were standing around the airport watching television and we found out the persian gulf war started when we were on the plane I guess. I'm glad our plane wasn't shot down or something. We rented a car, it was a great car. And then went to our hotel wich had vallet parking, it was beautiful. We went up to our hotel room and soon went to sleep.

The next morning when I woke up I took a shower and then came out, got dressed, and listened to what was going to happen today. My mom didn't have a meeting so we dicided to go to the Magic Kingdom. It was fantastic! We got there early and stood in this line that was about 12,000 feet long.

Finally we got in. We took the ferry across to the Magic Kingdom and were droped off there. And the day began!

Well not quite knowing where to begin, we went right into Fantasyland! It was cool, the first thing we went on was Snow White's Adventure my mom sat with me and it was scary (well back then it was, but now it isn't). My sister screched and had the time of her life, while I cried my eyes out the whole time, the only time I opened my eyes was at the end. We were going trough a diamond mine, the dwarves' diamond mine to be exact, and then we were about to leave and it looked like this huge diamond was going to fall on us! Then we left and went to a candy store. My mom got me a candy cane to calm me down. Then we went on this ride called Toad's Wild Ride that was cool. You see you got into these little cars and drove trough toad hall. It was fun and wild! Then we got onto this teacup ride, my mom got sick to her stomach and then said not to turn the teacup, she had a weak stomach, but we payed no attention and turned it super fast! Soon though the ride came to an end and my sister, dad, and I laghed at my mom's expression. Then we chose a more soothing ride called Pan's Flight, it was nifty. We got into these pirate ships and flew over London and then Never Never Land. It was neat.

Afterwards we went to Frontier Land and went

on the ride the haunted mansion wich was not too scary. Outside there were these funny tombstone like Here lies poor Fred a rock fell on his head. Then we went inside and rode this elevator that as we went down then there were these goofy pitures of how people coud die. Then we got into this little car thing and there was this guy who talked to us about the haunted mansion. His voice came over a speaker in the car. Then we went trough the haunted mansion. We my mom and I were in the same car and my sister and dad were ahead of us we saw these ghost skeletons playing in a band and once we came they wen't back into there grave. And then there were ghost eating at a table and when we came in they all flew up to the celling. Then we went into the library and there was a wich who's head was in a crystal bulb and ghost were flying all around it was creepy. Finally we reached the end and right before the ride was over there was something about hithiking ghost. We passed this mirror and looked in there was a big fat ghost who we picked up along our ride! It was so funny. I left wondering how they did that.

After wards we had lunch at Cinderalla's castle wich was cool because she showed up!

Then we went around taking pitures on main street and then went shoping for souviners. After that we went to Tommorwland. It was boring so we left quickly.

Then went into Adventureland we went in the Swiss Family Robionsin tree house. Wich was of course totally awesome we went on the ride 20000 leages under the sea wich was my favorite ride and this ride that was really cool but I forgot the name. After that we got ice cream and went shopping some more souviners. Soon the day came to an end. We my family lined up on main street and saw a parade and then we saw a fireworks display. Afterwards we rode the monirail to the parking lot.

The next day my mom had a meeting the whole day so my dad sister and I went to Epcot alone. Soon we left and went to Epcot once we arrived we walked around to all these differnt countires well they were mopre like lands. When we went to Canada we saw this movie and it felt like the room was moving.

There really weren't that many rides. Soon we went to Norway and got on this ride about some troll. It was a god awful ride.

Finally things got better we went to france and found this candy we really liked. And then we meet this guy and he had worked there before he told us a lot about the place. Then we went on this communications ride that was in the big golf ball. The best ride we went on it 3 times one right after the other becase no one was in line. Then we went trough the other countries and then walked around. At night fall we went home.

The next day my mom had a meeting in the morning.

ROAD TO NASHVILLE, ROAD TO MEMPHIS

"The name of the tune is 'Mississippi Goddam,'" Nina Simone declared ominously to her audience in 1965, "and I mean every word of it." Ida started to sing along and turned to Linnet and Rosalind in the backseat.

"Okay, when she gets to the words 'Mississippi Goddam' I want to hear you guys shout it out."

Nothing could have pleased them more than the prospect of yelling a profane word at the top of their lungs and even being given permission by their mother to say it in her presence.

"And everybody knows about MISSISSIPPI GODDAM," they sang out, tickled with the naughtiness of it all.

"What's she singing about?" Rosalind asked. "I mean, who is she talking about when she says, 'You all gonna die and die like flies'? Who's going to die and why?"

"It's a song about the civil-rights movement," Ida said. "Black folks were marching for their rights, sitting in at lunch counters, protesting, especially in the South. Nina's singing, at that point, about the white folk dying because they are such hypocrites, because they wanted to do anything to keep us from getting our fair share in this country."

"Yeah, I know about that," Linnet chimed in. "We learn about it every January when it's Martin Luther King's birthday. Rosa Parks and the Montgomery Bus Boycott. We watch *Eyes on the Prize.*"

"You remember last year," Ida continued, "when we went to the National Civil Rights Museum in Memphis? Well, Nina Simone is singing about that time."

The museum had been the very first stop we made when we exited from the interstate. The children and I walked together, with me remarking about exhibits here and there, an observation about Freedom Summer, another about the lunch-counter sit-ins, a bit on the March on Washington, a brief lecture on Martin Luther King, Jr.'s final days. My children are used to this. Indeed, they expect it. After all, their father is a professor who deals with this stuff, so while they only half-listen to the talk, they would be, in some sense, disappointed if I said nothing. They found the museum interesting but no more so than our trips to the Daniel Boone House, or the Hermitage, or Lincoln's grave. Ida had walked through the museum alone, something I hadn't noticed until we arrived at the end of the tour. Ida stood looking at the spot where King fell, and began to cry.

"Why are you crying, Mommy?" Rosalind asked. "Why are you crying?"

I was surprised too.

"I didn't think a retelling of the King story would move you like that," I said after we left the museum.

"I grew up in Dallas," she said quietly, "and there was a washeteria near my house that had a sign in the window that said 'Whites Only.' I saw signs that said 'No Colored' and 'No Colored Allowed.' But that washeteria always stayed with me because it was right there in my neighborhood. You didn't grow up with that. I did. I don't think anybody in my family thought those signs were going to come down in our lifetime."

The next morning we went to Graceland.

"It was very hard and dangerous work," I added to Ida's explanation about the marches, "and

Mississippi was a particularly backward and violent state. The white folk down there were murdering civil-rights workers left and right. I was a teenager during those years. It was all very exciting and heroic. You know, a black DJ in Philadelphia was fired for playing 'Mississippi Goddam' on the air, supposedly for violating FCC rules of playing a song with an obscenity. But he blipped the obscenity from the record. He was fired because of the song's sentiments.

"My oldest sister belonged to SNCC, the Student Non-Violent Coordinating Committee. I don't remember, maybe it was during Freedom Summer in 1965 that she joined. She brought a whole lot of music in the house during those years. Buffy St. Marie, Oscar Brown, Jr., lots of stuff, and this record by Nina Simone. She used to blast it from a tiny hi-fi we had and the surrounding neighborhood would be drenched by Nina Simone. I wonder what our Italian neighbors thought of it all."

"Did they get mad?" Linnet asked. "Did they tell you not to play it?"

"No," I said. "They never said anything about it. They never treated us any differently either. We always got along with them very well. That was a point of pride with my mother. They were strange years, though, the 1960s."

"Which sister was this," Rosalind wanted to know, "the one who comes to visit us sometimes? The mother of Hathor and Aminta? Not the one I'm named after, is it?"

"Well, you're named after both of my sisters. Your middle name is Lenora. Yes, and she is the mother of Hathor and Aminta and she is the one who comes to visit and she is the one who once belonged to SNCC."

"Oh, she's weird," Rosalind said. "No offense, I mean."

"No weirder than the rest of us, but you have a right to your opinion," I responded. A right to have your own opinion, not to have to follow the crowd, is something I have always felt strongly about, and so I have never missed an opportunity to tell either of them that.

We listened to the entire *Nina Simone in Concert* tape. The girls liked "Old Jim Crow," "Don't Smoke in Bed," and "Mississippi Goddam." They found "Pirate Jenny" from Weill and Brecht's *Threepenny Opera* puzzling.

"That's a crazy old song," Linnet said.

"At the time, lots of black folk thought it was a song about the black revolution, about overturning the system. My sisters played it all the time. You know, a lot of those songs that my sisters used to play come back to me now."

"Uh-oh, here comes a stroll down memory lane," Rosalind said.

I started to sing a folk song called "I Ain't A-Marching Anymore" by a guy named Phil Ochs, the anti-war anthem of my generation. That is, I fumbled about with the lyrics for a bit, trying to remember how it went, what wars were covered, thought there was a line about "set off the mighty mushroom roar" and "United Fruit streams at the Cuban shore." Or did United Fruit scream at the Cuban shore?

"Give us a break, Daddy," Rosalind started laughing. "You're worse than Cynthia's dad who's always singing Beatles songs when he drives carpool."

"This was the great popular music of America," I intoned with a bit of professorial gravity.

"Yeah, right," Rosalind said, "I never heard of this stuff."

"It was great music for the people back in the 1960s, like Daddy," Linnet said. "All the parents think that great music stopped when they had kids."

Rosalind gave Linnet five for that particular cutting remark.

"Okay, Daddy. Can it. Don't sing any more. We get the idea," Linnet wisecracked. But now the song was coming back to me in full. I was in rare good form.

"Save it for the shower," Rosalind suggested.

"Your father knows the white and black side of the street," Ida said, laughing. "I never heard of that song. But I didn't grow up around Italians, so my range of appreciation is not as wide as that."

"Yes, that's right," I laughed. "I was the only black kid in the neighborhood who preferred the Everly Brothers' version of 'Bye Bye Love' over Ray Charles's. Little Oreo me."

"Okay," she said. "Let's hear some Motown."

In goes another tape and the Supremes have the floor with "Where Did Our Love Go?"

And Ida and the girls are swaying in unison to the music, Ida lip-synching Diana Ross and the girls doing Mary Wilson and Florence Ballard. Our van zipped down the road, the motor humming, the tires cushioning the road, and the Earlys singing away in the car. We were on our way to Nashville. Then, in quick succession, came Stevie Wonder's "Uptight," Marvin Gaye's "Stubborn Kind of Fellow," the Temptations' "I Know I'm Losing You" and Martha and the Vandellas' "Dancing In the Street."

Summer's here and the time is right...

"Now," I said to Linnet and Rosalind, when

Martha and the Vandellas faded out, "that was the song of the revolution. That song came out in 1964, just when black folk started rioting in northern cities and folk started saying that the song was about revolution, was about encouraging black folk to go into the streets and change the system."

"Well, was it?" Rosalind asked.

"No, it wasn't. Those poor girls who made that record were shocked to find out that people were hearing the song that way. They said something to the effect, 'What's wrong with these crazy niggers out here? We ain't talking about no riots.'" Linnet and Rosalind cracked up at that. I changed tapes.

"I lost someone," the singer began.

"Your father loves his James Brown," Ida said.

"Well, I don't," Rosalind said.

"Gee whiz, I love you," Brown pleaded.

"How much of this James Brown we got to listen to? I'm with Ros," Ida said, after a few more minutes of my lip-synching.

The tape hissed on and the Godfather of Soul, the Hardest-Working Man in Show Business Today, The Man Who Never Left sang "Hot Pants, Parts I and II," "Funky President," "Escapism, Part I and II," "Stone to the Bone," and "Money Won't Change You."

Finally, I popped in a blues tape. It was where I wanted to arrive, not where I wanted to end, as I drove into Nashville.

"I was waiting for this," Ida said. "The trip back to the primal."

It was Howling Wolf.

"Somebody's calling me," Wolf shouted into the Chess Studio microphone, his brooding 250 pounds hardly containable in that studio, on the tape, in the car, in fact, could only be contained, held, realized, by life itself. I opened up the window, despite the fact we had the air-conditioning running, to give the great Wolf more room, as he was liable to run me and the whole family out of the car. I thought of the famous blues from the turn of the century:

> I thought I heard Buddy Bolden shout
> Open up the window and let the bad air out

"This, kids, is the blues," I said.

They were both silent.

"We heard them before," Rosalind said, finally. "You play them all the time, when you're not playing jazz or some string quartet by somebody or other. Besides, we heard this stuff in Memphis last summer all over Beale Street." Muddy sang "Sad Letter" and B. B.

sang "Sweet Sixteen" and Mississippi John Hurt sang "Louis Collins."

My brother's in Korea, baby (and I thought about my uncle's picture at my grandmother's house, dressed and framed in his army uniform, looking as young and fearless, as serious and motivated, as any soldier, and when my mother took me to see Sidney Poitier in "All the Young Men" in 1960, I thought of my uncle, for it was the first time I had seen on a movie screen a black man as the hero of a war movie, and I thought that, perhaps, it may have been the story of my uncle in Korea).

Dark was the night, cold was the ground (and I thought of the burial of my cousin, Geno, shot in a street-gang war just a few steps from his house, when a picture of the night of the shooting, his falling to the cold, unrelenting ground, came to me, would not leave me, although I wanted to shake it all off like veritable dust).

"Your father loves his blues," Ida smiled. "Let's indulge him."

Perhaps I love them because the attitude toward life expressed in blues records—that everyone has troubles but they can be endured, that happiness is not lasting, so don't be fooled by your good times—is truly the essence of "blackness." Blues do not promise that people will not be unhappy, but that unhappiness can be transcended, not by faith in God, but by faith in one's own ability to accept unhappiness without ever conceding oneself to it. Blackness is not an Afrocentric lesson, nor a coming together of the tribe in fake unity. It is this: a fatalistic, realistic belief in human transcendence, born in the consciousness of a people who experienced the gut-wrenching harshness of slavery, of absorbing the absolute annihilation of their humanity, and who lived to tell the world and their former masters about it. And it is about how they reinvented their humanity in the meanwhile. The blues was the only thing I ever consciously used to try to teach my children about black people, whether it was Charlie Parker's blues or Mississippi John Hurt's blues. It was, oddly, the only thing I ever wanted really to tell them about being black in America or in the world, for that matter. The rest of my blackness, from Kemet to Du Bois, could be washed away from me tomorrow with nary a sigh for its passing. But not the blues. I felt that black people should not be remembered for being geniuses, founding civilizations, creating cultures, or any of the other things they/we have done. Black people should be remembered for being wise and tough, and that was, in the end, the most that could be said of any people. And that is what I wanted my daughters to be: wise and tough. Moreover, I wanted them to feel truly and deeply what they felt and not have either blacks or whites tell them how they were supposed to feel or what they were supposed to feel as blacks. The blues taught that, too: be nobody but yourself.

I closed the windows of the van with the buttons on my left. The car was starting to get hot and blowy. I was wasting the air conditioning and it was hard to hear the music over the road noise. Of course, as Ralph Ellison wrote, old Louis Armstrong himself wouldn't have thrown out the bad air because "it would have broken up the music and the dance."

"I like the blues," Linnet said, suddenly, quietly.

We were, not surprisingly, the only black people on the Graceland tour.

"Do you think they get very many black people to take this tour?" I whispered to Ida.

"I doubt it," Ida said, purposely not whispering, "But they hit the jackpot today. Four nutty Negroes down here touring the home of a white man who was imitating a Negro who was some white man's idea to begin with. Only in America."

The tour itself was a disappointment.

"This house is so small," said Linnet, as we walked through the rooms, a docent telling us all about the home of this strange man, of our true bewildered Citizen Kane and his Xanadu. "I thought Graceland would be much bigger."

"And the man had no taste," Ida said, "He's got just the kind of home you'd expect some poor guy from Mississippi to have once he got a little money."

"You say that like you hate the guy," I said.

"Hate him? Are you kidding? I feel sorry for him. This is pathetic. A basement room full of mirrors and that hideous Jungle Room, and the whole house looks like the furniture came from the places that sell furniture to our parents."

"You're sounding like a middle-class snob," I said.

"It takes one to know one," she answered.

We toured everything—the museums across the street from the mansion itself, the planes, the cars; saw all manner of Elvis home movies. We took the deluxe package. When we finished Ida said she never wanted to hear another word about Elvis Presley for the rest of her life. Lin-

net and Rosalind seemed bored and oppressed
and glad we were, at last, leaving, after having
spent more than four hours at Graceland.
There was a great sense, while there, of being
inside a tomb, of being within something
embalmed and mummified and petrified like
some kind of taxidermist's absurdist fantasy.
One could easily imagine a stuffed, mounted
Elvis watching over you. And after hearing
how Elvis supported so many people, how he
put the city of Memphis on the map, how he
endured being virtually trapped by his fame, by
his whims and fancies, his entourage and his
possessions (and he was, like the true American
lord of consumption that was consumed, nothing more than his possessions, in some measure), there was an overwhelming sense,
indeed, that one had seen the garish shrine of
a pale, lesser, tormented prince. We stood, at
the very end of the tour, looking at his and his
mother's graves. It was raining heavily and I
had given my umbrella to the children. As I was
being drenched by the rain, I heard a woman
blow her nose. I turned and saw another crying. Most people looked reverent, respectful.
The four of us stood there, exchanging side
glances, and I think, for one moment, at least, a
raw kind of telepathy passed through us and

gravity. And when I turned toward what I supposed was the commons or quadrangle of some sort, the campus looked collegiatelike and pretty enough. I sat on a bench. I suppose I must have looked a bit perplexed or dementedly beguiled.

"What do you want to do, Daddy?" Linnet asked.

I looked at her. She seemed a little worried about me, as if I were worried about having to come to this place to write a book about it, and perhaps she was more than a little afraid for her father to be in a strange place, on a campus that did not look like the campus and environs of Washington University, where her parents worked—lush, suburban, and cloistered from everything but its own reality.

I touched her hand. "Why don't we come back tomorrow when this place is open and find the place where the Fisk Jubilee Singers sang? That's what we came for," I grinned. And she grinned too, relieved that her father had a grip of the situation, a purpose, a reason for all of us being there.

"Well, where will we go next summer?" Ida asked, the van tires springing on the road, the sun fading into a darkening haze of light and gold, burnt and washed out. From the tape player, just barely audible, Miles Davis's late-1950s sextet was playing, while Ida, in shorts and sneakers, gripped the wheel and I sat on the passenger side, shaded, pensive, quiet.

"I know where!" Linnet burst out. "New York. Let's go to New York next summer."

"No," Rosalind countered, "I want to go to Washington, D.C. Then, let's go to Orlando and Disney World."

"We've been to Disney World," I reminded Rosalind.

"So, what's wrong with going again? Is there some law against it?"

"No, there isn't. But it's dumb to go back," Linnet said. "I don't want to go there. New York is much better. Besides, I'm going to Washington with my eighth-grade class and I don't want to go again next summer on a family vacation."

"Who cares about you and your stinky old eighth-grade class?" Rosalind retorted. "People get murdered in New York. Let's go to Washington."

I said that people get murdered in Washington, too, and then told them where I thought we should go.

"Beverly, New Jersey!?" Rosalind shouted.

"What's in Beverly, New Jersey?" Linnet asked.

"My father is buried in Beverly, New Jersey," I said. "I have never seen his grave. My father, your grandfather. I have no idea what condition it's in. But next year we are going to find his grave and we are going to fix it up. Maybe put a marker or monument on it. I've got to do that. I'm ashamed I never did it when I was younger."

"Why didn't your mother do it?" Rosalind suddenly chimed. For a moment, the question irritated me, probably because I could not rightly answer it. Maybe my mother ignored my father's grave because she never had any money to do anything for it. Maybe she never liked my father or maybe at the time he died their relationship had soured. It occurred to me that I knew no one in my father's family.

"Only your father's brother came to his funeral," my mother said. "They didn't seem interested in him. So I never bothered with them."

I turned to Rosalind. "He was only my mother's husband. He wasn't her father."

There was a long respectful silence in the van. Ida squeezed my arm for a moment.

"Well, okay, Daddy," Rosalind said. "But after we go to New Jersey and be sad and serious, can we go to New York and have fun?"

PART III

HOME:
"THE RISING OF THE SUN
AND THE RUNNING
OF THE DEER"

"I was thinking," he answered absently, "about Euripides; how, when he was an old man, he went and lived in a cave by the sea, and it was thought queer, at the time. It seems that houses had become insupportable to him. I wonder whether it was because he had observed women so closely all his life."

—The Professor in Willa Cather's
The Professor's House

One should be eternally feminine.

—E. Azalia Hackley,
The Colored Girl Beautiful

The Worst Christmas

"The worst Christmas we had," Rosalind began, "was back a few years ago when everybody got sick on Christmas Eve and Mommy couldn't cook Christmas dinner and we were all barfing and moaning in bed. And on Christmas morning, we opened up our stuff, looked at it for a minute, then when to back to bed for the rest of the day. Wow, what a rotten Christmas!"

Probably we all had a mild case of food poisoning. We had gone to McDonald's to have an early lunch on Christmas Eve. (We had not eaten any breakfast.) By late afternoon, one by one, each of us was stricken. First, Rosalind took to her bed, vomiting, with chills, suddenly weakened as if a genie had magically drained all her Christmas energy and excitement from her. Then I became very ill, although I still tried to go around with as much Christmas cheer as I could.

"It's just a little indigestion. I'll be all right in a few hours," I told Ida, who was in the kitchen preparing the big feast for tomorrow.

"Men never want to admit when they're sick," Ida said, laughing. "Why don't you go to bed?"

Soon, Linnet was down, writhing and retch-
ing. And, finally, late in the afternoon, the pots
were silent, the ingredients of various dishes
left upon the counter in midpreparation, the
kitchen deserted, as Ida lay in bed, pale and
trembling.

"What's wrong with us?" she asked weakly
from the covers, piled on the bed as if it were
one of the coldest days of the year. (It was,
indeed, a very warm Christmas Eve, as mild as
any I could ever remember.) "What do we
have? A stomach virus?"

"I doubt if we would all catch a stomach
virus on the same day, at nearly the same hour.
It's probably food poisoning."

"Oh, God," Ida groaned, "this is going to
wreck our Christmas. I'm too sick to finish dinner. I can't even finish wrapping the gifts."

Although I was sick, I tried very hard to
keep everyone's spirits up, telling jokes, singing
Christmas songs—"Now, here's my imitation
of Nat King Cole and here's my imitation of
Bing Crosby and here's my imitation of Louis
Armstrong..." "Hey, Daddy, why don't you try
imitating silence?" "Ahh, an ungrateful, unap-
preciative audience here. What a great artist
must endure from his public"—trying desperately to keep Christmas alive and well. But

alas, it dissipated, hopelessly. What kind of holiday atmosphere can you have when people are regurgitating after taking a sip of water!

"I'll never eat at McDonald's again," Linnet said disgustedly.

"Promises, promises," I chimed. "But we aren't certain that it was the food from McDonald's that made us sick. I'll bet you'll eat at McDonald's again before the New Year."

"Never," she said.

I won that bet.

By early evening, everyone had fallen into a restless sleep. I awoke at about ten or so and was aware that the food for tomorrow's meal had not been put away. As I put away the sweet potatoes, the turkey, the half-finished dressing, the pie crust, the bags of vegetables, I thought that I might finish the dinner myself. I was, after all, the regular cook of the house, just as my father had been in his house. "I never cooked until after your father died," my mother told me once. "He was a much better cook than I was and besides he liked cooking. I never liked it." Ida only cooked for the holidays, and the recipes were all spread out on the kitchen table. But I felt a bit too weak to attempt it. Some of the gifts aren't done, I thought. I'd better get to them.

I brought up the few remaining gifts from

the basement, sat by the tree with the wrapping paper, tape, and scissors, and started on the work. The house was completely silent, eerily so. It did not feel like Christmas, whatever Christmas is supposed to feel like. I had been working in a rather self-absorbed way for many minutes when, suddenly, feeling another presence, I turned and saw Rosalind standing there, blanket and pillow dragging the floor.

"You scared the living daylights out of me," I said.

"I couldn't sleep anymore. Then I saw there was a light on."

"You aren't supposed to be up on Christmas Eve. Besides, I am trying to wrap these gifts. You shouldn't be up. You'll see the stuff before it's wrapped."

"That's okay. I'll just sit on the sofa and not look." And that is exactly what she did.

I continued until all the gifts were done.

"Are you feeling any better? Can I get you something?" I asked.

"I'm a little better. I don't want anything. I'll just throw it up."

"A pretty lousy Christmas, huh?" I ventured.

"Yeah, not so good. I can't enjoy anything, I feel so bad. It wouldn't be so bad if everybody else wasn't sick, too."

We hung fire for a time.

"Why aren't you asleep, Daddy?"

"I couldn't sleep. I have never been able to sleep on Christmas Eve night since I was a boy."

"What was Christmas like for you as a boy, Daddy?"

I considered the question for a moment. "It was a wonderful time. My mother would have the house smelling real good and there were bowls of hard candy, nuts, and oranges all around the house. I couldn't believe how much bounty there was in the house at Christmas. Especially the oranges. I loved the oranges. They were a special treat. I couldn't stop eating them and even as I ate them more would appear as if by magic. It was as if we would never run out of food. When I was older I was so amazed at this because we were as poor as church mice. My sisters and I would decorate the tree and my mother would cook and prepare the house by stringing up Christmas cards and stuff like that. My mother would take me to visit the department-store Santa Claus and my sisters would take me to a store called Lit Brothers to see their Christmas village and then we would go to another store called Wanamaker's to hear carols played on a huge organ and hear a choir sometimes. What I liked most about Christmas was that my oldest sister, Lenora, would be very kind to me. She's five years older than I am and when we were children she thought I was just a little pest, a nuisance. But at Christmas, for some reason, she would be very kind and thoughtful. Once she read to me Dickens's *A Christmas Carol*. I don't know why she did. But she read it very beautifully and I could have listened to her forever. That was the same Christmas I got a little toy that all the boys wanted that year, called the Great Garloo. It was little robot thing that operated by remote control, built in the shape of an imp or genie or something like that. It was advertised as the toy that could be your personal slave. I guess toy companies wouldn't advertise a toy like that nowadays. Another time my sister read *The Wizard of Oz,* the whole book, in the few days before and after Christmas. And always her younger sister, Rosalind, would play the piano in the evening, some Christmas carols and songs from the *Nutcracker* Suite and the Anna Magdelena Notebook. At night, we would go to midnight Mass at St. Mary's Episcopal Church. The church would be very beautiful for Christmas Mass, with wreaths and incense, and the night was always crisp and full of stars. In those days, we would go to church for Christmas Mass on the bus. Can you believe it? No one would do that now. One year, after I had become an altar boy, I was the thurifer for the Christmas Mass and that was one of the most lovely moments of my life."

"What's a thurifer?" Rosalind asked.

"The altar boy who handles the censer and leads the procession into church."

We were quiet for a bit. Then, to fill the silence, I decided to play a record of Christmas carols sung by some church choir. The volume was low, so no sleeping ones would be disturbed.

> The holly and the ivy
> When they are both full grown
> Of all the trees that are in the wood
> The holly bears the crown.

"That's your favorite Christmas carol, isn't it, Daddy?" Rosalind asked, weakly. She was losing her strength. She would be asleep soon.

"Yes," I said. "I heard it played for the first time in my life as a boy on a church organ. It just touched me deeply and the words touched me too."

I moved to the sofa and started to rub Rosalind's feet through the blanket. I felt such an urge to throw up that I could hardly refrain from doing so. I fought the bile back down because, somehow, to me, it seemed inappropriate, wrong, to be sick on Christmas. I could feel the sweat on my forehead from the effort.

"Christmas with a house of sick women, and I'm sick myself," I said, turning to Rosalind.

But she was already, head turned aside, mouth slightly open, fast asleep.

"This Machine Kills Fascists"

...in this white-man world you got to take yuh mouth and make a gun.

—Florrie in Paule Marshall's
Brown Girl, Brownstones

It might be said that I ran the risk of living a completely uneventful life, of being able to avoid even the most remote possibility of ever being notorious or an object of scrutiny. But the town of Frontenac, a suburb of St. Louis, saved me from such a fate, and for two weeks in November in 1991, I was probably the most talked-about man in St. Louis.

The cause of this was simple enough: Ida, an officer in the Junior League, took me and the children to a Junior League Christmas bazaar

at Le Chateau Mall, which was where the
Junior League headquarters was located then.
While she and the girls looked at the Christmas
displays, I, bored and restless, walked around
the mall for a bit then went back to our van
and sat there for a time and read. After twenty
or thirty minutes, I went back through the mall
to get them. I walked past a jewelry store. A
man and a woman stood in front of it, talking.
I didn't say anything to them, never stopped
to look at anything in the jewelry store, barely
even glanced at them. I simply wanted to get
home. None of us had eaten dinner. I was fairly
hungry by this point, and we had promised the
kids their favorite: pizza.

When I arrived back at the Junior League
headquarters, I couldn't find Ida or the kids.
Once again, I went down the front steps of the
Junior League and stood there, waiting for
them to come out. Then the adventure began.
A young police officer named Mayer drove up
and asked me what I was doing there. He told
me that he had received a call with a description of someone who looked like me "lurking"
in the mall. Something in me snapped. There I
was, I immediately thought, about to be humiliated before the whites coming in and out of
the building (and there were a good many of

them doing so, through the front entrance), being reminded that I was a nigger, that I had no business being where I was, that I was a "threat" to the good white folk of Frontenac.

"You want identification," I said, flinging my wallet at him. "Here's mountains of identification. Take your pick."

He refused to pick it up, so I bent over, picked it up, and put it on the hood of his car.

"What's in your pocket?" he asked ominously. I had been holding one hand in my pocket since his arrival. I took off my jacket, flung it on the car, dumped the contents of my pocket on the hood of his car, and spread-eagled for him.

"I don't want you to have any reason to kill me," I said. "Besides, we all know that we're going through this little drama because of my race."

"Your race has nothing to do with this," Officer Mayer told me.

"Well, there are plenty of white guys 'lurking' around here and nobody's stopping them."

At that point both Ida and the kids came out.

"Come on, Jer, let's go," she called.

"I can't go anywhere," I said. "This police officer is trying to see if I am a dangerous criminal."

Ida dropped her purchases on the front steps

of the league, left the children, and ran over to Officer Mayer.

"What are you doing?" she shouted. "What are you doing? This is my husband. He hasn't done anything. What the hell are you doing?"

"We got a call about a person lurking in the mall who fit your husband's description…" Officer Mayer began.

"What call?" Ida asked frantically. "Who called? Who made that call?"

By this time, Officer Mayer had finished running my driver's license through the computer check and had given it back to me. I picked up my jacket and belongings and walked back to the kids, who were completely nonplussed about what was going on. I picked up Ida's purchases, took the kids by the arm, and we sat on the steps in front of the league, waiting while Ida angrily argued with the officer, who kept insisting that he was merely doing his job.

"What's going on, Daddy?" Linnet asked.

"The police stopped me for questioning and an I.D. check," I said.

"But why? You hadn't done anything."

"I guess because I looked like somebody who might do something," I said, holding my head in my hands.

"I can't believe this," Ida said as we were driving home. "I can't believe this. Who would call the cops? I don't understand this."

"Maybe one of your Junior Leaguers who was scared by the big bad Negro man," I said.

"They wouldn't do that. They wouldn't do something like that. I just can't believe one of them would do something like that."

"Well, somebody did," I said, "and that's that. Let's just chalk this up as an inevitable embarrassment you experience from time to time being black and call it a day. I just want to forget the whole business."

No one ate much dinner that night.

Although I was ready to forget the whole affair, Ida was not. The next morning she told me she wanted to see the chief of police in Frontenac and get an apology for what happened.

"Just forget about it," I said. "They aren't going to give you an apology. For what? A guy who didn't get arrested and who didn't get his head beaten in? Why, that chief of police is just going to look at you and say, 'Why, your husband is one lucky nigger as far as I can tell. He ain't in jail and he's still in one piece.'"

"No," Ida said adamantly. "This wasn't right, and I'm going to see somebody about it."

"Okay, okay, listen. Since I can't talk you out of it, don't go see anybody without calling me first. I'll go with you."

When I arrived at school that day, I ran into my friend Wayne Fields, then the chair of the English department, and I told him the story, almost jocularly now. I had gotten over the whole business. It seemed a small thing to worry about.

"Listen," Wayne said, "I'm going to call the *Post-Dispatch*. I know a guy down there and I'm going to have this written up. This stuff has got to stop."

I was almost instantly sorry I had told Wayne. I'm not telling a reporter about this, I thought. This is too ridiculous for words. It's no big deal. I just won't call him back and he'll forget about it by this afternoon. I also thought that by the time Ida was on the job, busy with the day-to-day stuff at the office, she, too, would forget about it.

At around four in the afternoon, I finally reached Ida. I had tried her several times earlier in the day without success. Since she hadn't called me, I figured that she had simply changed her mind about seeing the police chief of Frontenac.

"Where have you been?" I asked. "I've been trying you all day."

"Oh, out driving," she said thickly. Her voice sounded tight and strange, as if she had been crying.

"Out driving where?" I asked.

"I don't know, Gerald, just anywhere. I don't know. I don't know where I've been. I've just been driving." She started crying into the phone.

"Ida, what happened?" I asked. "Were you hurt or injured or something?"

"No, I went to see...the chief of police of Frontenac. Some guy named, named, I think, Ben Branch," she said, trying to control her sobbing.

"I told you not to go out there unless you called me first. I told you not to go see those people without me," I said angrily.

"No, Gerald, it was better this way. It was safer for you. That's why I went by myself. It was better that way. I thought they wouldn't feel as threatened just facing a woman."

"Well, what happened?" I asked anxiously.

"Oh, Gerald, it was awful. He just sat there defending his police officer. He didn't care. To him, you were just a nigger who was in the wrong place at the wrong time. I was just sitting there listening to all this. I just started crying and crying. I couldn't control myself and I was so ashamed because I didn't want to cry in front of this man. But I couldn't help it. He was killing me, Gerald. Everything he was saying. The way he acted. He was just killing me as if he were shooting me with bullets. They don't see us as human beings. We're just, I don't know, just some kind of animal or something. He kept saying that the officer followed procedure. I told him the officer humiliated you in front of all those people, all those white people, in front of your own children. But he didn't care. Then, finally, he played the tape of the call they received. It was the jeweler in the mall, and you should have heard the way he described you. He said you were "casing the joint" and that it was obvious you were planning a robbery. He said the white woman who was there was afraid to go to her car after seeing you. I just started crying all over again.

"Well, I left there and decided to see this jeweler. I just couldn't believe he would make this call and say those awful things about you. And I went to see him and he was worse than Branch. He said, 'Your husband must not be much of man, sending you out to get his apologies. And what's so special about your husband anyway? I've been stopped before. If he hadn't done anything, why should he mind? Maybe you guys were afraid because you were trying to hide something.' I just couldn't believe the ugly things he said. But I wouldn't cry in front of him. No, not him. But he was killing me too. But I wouldn't cry.

"Then, I left his store and I don't know what I did. I was crying in the car for I don't know how long. I couldn't go back to work because I couldn't stop crying. Then, I started driving, just anywhere. Just driving and crying. I'm surprised I wasn't killed in an accident. Finally, I got back to work just a few minutes ago.

"I'm sorry I didn't tell you. But it was better this way. Especially with that jeweler. He was so hateful and racist."

I was quiet for so long that Ida had to ask to see if I was still on the line.

"I'll call you back," I said.

I called Wayne and told him what Ida had said. As I talked I was finding it harder and harder to control my voice. I could feel myself breaking down.

"And she was crying, Wayne, crying so much. She was crying more about this than over anything I've ever done to her," I said, trying to make a joke but failing miserably.

"They think I'm some kind of animal, that they can do whatever they want to me," I said, and now to my astonishment, I was crying too.

"They think I'm an animal and that Ida is nothing more than the wife of an animal. *I am not
an animal!*" I shouted. "*I am not an animal. I
am not an animal.*" My head was on the desk
and I was crying to one of my colleagues.
Wayne was trying to calm me down. I was silent
for a time, pulling myself together. I said at last:

"If you can get hold of that reporter, I'm
willing to talk."

Once the story broke, the next two weeks were
the most stressful and trying of my life. At first,
Ida and I considered the story minor, just a bit
of publicity to embarrass Frontenac, the jeweler,
and the police. But the local press decided the
story about a black professor versus the lily-
white, affluent town of Frontenac was too rich to
let go. Bigger stories followed. Interviews on the
television news. "Will the W.U. Professor
Stopped and Questioned by Frontenac Police
Get His Apology?" I hadn't been aware that that
was even what I was after until the news stories
told me. The jeweler tried to put a different spin
on things by saying that I was actually standing
in front of his store, looking at his merchandise.

"That's a damn lie," I told Ida. "Anybody
who knows me knows I don't like jewelry,

never wear it, and would never be caught dead in a jewelry store or even window-shopping for jewelry. Remember how mad you were when I lost our wedding ring two weeks after we were married? That's how much I dislike jewelry."

"Forget it, Gerald. Don't get into a fight about whether you were actually standing in front of the store. That's what he would want. That would play to his advantage. We both know it's a lie but it doesn't matter."

Ida and I began to receive hate mail. This too made her cry. We were attacked on the editorial page by a variety of police officers who said I was "arrogant" and the like. The *Post-Dispatch* countered by running an editorial supporting us. But after about a week or so, I felt I had to issue some sort of statement and take some sort of definitional control over the matter. One Friday, I taped to my PC the words "This Machine Kills Fascists" and started writing my own op-ed piece.

"What does that mean, Daddy?" Rosalind asked. "'This Machine Kills Fascists.'"

"It is something that the great folksinger Woody Guthrie used to write on his guitar. It means that I am going to use my words to slay all fascist and fascist-thinking people."

"Are fascists white people?"

"No," I said, "fascists are bad people. They can be any color and they have screwy ideas about race and blood. And when I get finished killing these white racist dogs, there are plenty of black fascists that need killing through words too." The piece that ran in the *Post-Dispatch* told readers that my stepfather was a retired police officer, that I was well aware of the hazards of the profession and was certainly not antipolice. But I went on to remind readers that despite my black skin, I was allowed free and equal access to all public places without compromise and without suspicion unless my actions clearly warranted such. Mere walking did not justify my having to give an account of myself to the police.

Some people at my church and at school started a letter-writing campaign on my behalf. I was on talk radio. The dean of the college, the provost, and the chancellor all called me to express concern about what happened. The Junior League rallied to my defense. I never knew I had so many friends, so many white friends at that. Many of the people who knew me and Ida were genuinely and deeply upset about what had happened. A white woman at my church came up to me after service one Sunday, rubbed my back tenderly, and said, her eyes welling with tears, "I'm so sorry about what happened to you. It's a disgrace to every white person in St. Louis." And, of course, I heard from black folk. Many called me at my office, often to recite more horrible encounters with the police than I had had. The local black newspaper did a big story about the incident. Yet I felt strange and uncomfortable, especially talking about it with blacks. I discovered, surprisingly, that the entire racial aspect of the incident embarrassed me, the call for racial solidarity, the demand for it, in effect, because of the incident, made me uneasy. I did not feel as though I was my brother's brother, truly, and becoming a racial firebrand or at least a symbol for racial justice made me often see myself, frankly, as a hypocrite. For many blacks, I was demanding an apology for the race itself, for all the untold number of times white police stopped and humiliated some poor black soul who had not done anything except live and be black. But at least a few saw through me as a race hero or made me feel more richly the alienation from my brothers and sisters that my education and my temperament had engendered. And their reactions made me feel my ambivalence about racial solidarity more acutely, for there was nothing I wanted more, nothing I yearned for more deeply than to be taken into the fold of blackness, and yet at the same time nothing that more appalled me, made me feel more imprisoned than the security blanket of racial isolation. O, to be a hero of the race for a mere hour! O, to be burdened by race at all!

"You know I appreciate what you're doing," a black male caller told me one afternoon. "But you know you can take the stand that you're taking because you won't lose your job. In fact, the white folks on your job see you as some kind of hero or symbol. And you have the backing of rich white folks. Because you know and I know that you could have the backing of every black person in this city and the white press and the white media wouldn't even be taking you seriously. I'm not trying to belittle what you're doing, but you're not a race man. You're just a black man with powerful white connections."

"I'm sorry if I've disappointed you," I told the caller, "but I'm not a race hero. And I'm not trying to be one." Yet the call wounded me deeply, stung me to the quick, for I had wanted to be seen in a bit better light than that.

On the other hand, Vernon, a black man who happens to be the custodian at my church, would just beam every time he saw me. "Yeah, Doc," he would say, "them folks out in Frontenac knowin' now you ain't a black man to mess around with. All the black folks I know are one hundred percent behind you. Especially because you ain't one of them big rabble-rousing race guys. Folks are proud 'cause you got a lot of education and you and your wife are doing this with a lot of dignity and not just callin' people racist. You a real role model, Doc."

"My teachers were talking about you at school today," Linnet told me one afternoon when she came home from school. "They think you're a hero and they hope you make Frontenac apologize."

"Do you think I'm a hero?" I asked.

"I don't know," she said somewhat distractedly, "I guess you're doing what you think you've got to do."

"I'm tired of the teachers asking me about you at school, Daddy," Rosalind said on another day. "I want to tell them that this is something you're doing, not me. I want to tell them that if they want to know about it, they should talk to you."

"Do you think I'm a hero?" I asked, with true anxiety in my voice.

"Do *you* think you're one, Daddy?" Rosalind shot back incredulously.

What I learned from this incident was this: that blackness has something to do with solidarity, with a sense of connection with other people who share your condition and with other people who could not possibly share your condition; and that blackness has nothing to do with solidarity, nothing to do with some idea we call race and is, finally, the exploration of the night within you, what Céline called "the depths of the night themselves," and that all other conceptions of blackness are merely distractions. This is what I hated about the Frontenac incident, not its punishing reality, but its unrelenting unreality. It was a brutalizing fantasy, a distraction of the most unrewarding kind. I was neither hero nor opportunist. I was simply a man caught up in some bemusing circumstances, "getting my head rubbed against a hard, grainy wall," someone once put it. For I should not have wanted the approval of black people, nor should I have seen myself as a pet of the whites and reveled in that privilege. I should have wanted justice simply for the sake of justice and because it would have pleased God for me to seek this on His behalf and in His name.

It was at this time, during the Frontenac trial, that I, worst card player in the world, tried to teach Linnet and Rosalind some card games with indifferent success. Linnet kept insisting that she wanted to learn how to play Pinochle because it was "a cool game with a cool name."

"I can't teach you that game," I said.

"Why not?" Linnet insisted. "Can't you just look up the rules in a card game book?"

"It's not that simple," I said. "I mean, the game is not that simple. When I was a boy, the guys would try to teach it to me. But they would be talking so fast and showing me all the stuff so quickly that I could never catch on. So, I kept getting my head rubbed. At first, they were amused by this but then they got bored and irritated. After a while, they said, 'We're dealing you out of this. You keep getting your head rubbed. You can't play. You just a chump, Jerry. You can't play.' It's just a game I could never understand. So, it doesn't matter about reading the rules. I just can't play that game."

❖

At last, there was a meeting set up for me and Ida and the mayor of Frontenac, Newell Baker, to settle the matter. I knew this gathering was not likely to go well when he started the meeting with some bad, anti-Catholic jokes about pigeons. Oh God, I thought, some white people truly have one type of mentality and that is idiocy. It never got any better as the mayor and his aide simply tried to tell me that nothing bad had happened to me. The police stop white people every day for the same sort of stuff. The mayor's position was that the police had acted properly, and this was true: the true culprit in this was the jeweler. But of course his action was understandable because it was reasonable for him to fear robbery. The jeweler's father had been, apparently, injured or killed in a holdup. But the jeweler's fears or the police officer's conduct was not, at last, the issue. The fact of the matter was that there were plenty of white men walking around that mall that night just as I was, and they weren't stopped in front of their families and questioned as suspicious characters. If they were good enough to pass muster as law-abiding citizens, then so was I. And the town of Frontenac owed me an apology on that basis: for not having treated me as it treats white men (and if we profess to live in a color-blind soci-

ety, that is precisely the treatment I want, the
same that is accorded to white men). The mayor
refused to see any aspect of the larger picture,
of the significance of what had happened, perhaps afraid that any concession on his part
would instigate a lawsuit. I felt like just walking out, telling the good mayor and his hench-
man that they could take their bullshit and
shove it back up their asses. Finally, after about
forty-five minutes of getting nowhere, Ida rose
and said that since the mayor was not willing
to apologize, we might as well leave as this was
a waste of everybody's time. It was then that the
mayor, obviously not wishing for us to go out
to reporters (a group of whom were waiting outside the door) and tell them of the city officials'
intransigence in this regard, came up suddenly
with a letter that said that Frontenac, well, sort
of apologized to those exceptional Negroes Ida
and Gerald Early, for making them feel uncomfortable and unwanted. It wasn't much, but it
was the most we were going to get.

But this small victory was not without its
considerable price. Ida and I were afraid to
drive anywhere in St. Louis for a time because
we felt we would be harassed by police officers sympathetic to Frontenac. We were afraid
to open our mail because of the hate mail we

were receiving. We were afraid to answer the phone because of the crank calls. I was so tense that I could scarcely sleep. I had little appetite. For Ida it was much the same. But more than anything else, these two weeks nearly wrecked my relationship with my children.

On the night the incident happened, Linnet was so upset that she went straight to bed.

"I think I'm getting a cold," she said.

And neither Linnet nor Rosalind wanted to talk about it. Every time it was broached to them, they wanted to change the subject, or they would simply listen quietly.

"I'll be glad when this is over," Rosalind said.

"Why?" I asked. "Because it is too stressful for you?"

"No," she said. "Because I'm tired of hearing about race."

Once, while she was lying in bed, still sick from something, I tried patiently to explain it all to Linnet.

"Do you know why I was stopped?" I asked.

"No, Daddy," she moaned, "I don't know. I mean, I don't understand."

"Well, because I'm a black man," I said, as if that made everything clear and self-evident.

"Oh," she said. "Do we have to talk about it? I don't feel that well."

"Yes," I said emphatically, "yes, we have to talk about it. You're used to being around these white folks and you think they mean you some good. But they don't mean you any good."

"Daddy, I'm tired, do we have to talk about it now?"

"Yes," I said, feeling myself becoming slowly, more hysterically angry, "yes, right now. Because I have to get these nutty notions out of your head about white folks."

"Daddy, I don't want to hear it," she said, her voice rising.

"I don't care what you want to hear. You're going to hear this now. Don't you know race runs this world?" I threw the blankets from her. I was losing control of myself entirely.

"Do you see this?" I grabbed her arm and held it. "This skin color? This is what deter-mines what goes on in this world. This, and only this. Nothing but this. Has never been anything but this."

"Daddy, stop this!"

"I'm your father and you're going to listen. You've gotten too cozy with these white folks but I'm going to get you out of that. It's time you understood about race, about being black. Your mother and I made a mistake trying to be nice, good Negroes, striving Negroes, liberal Negroes who were going to try to accept these white folk. Why, we thought we were too good to talk about race in this house like the common, complaining niggers do. No sir, we were enlightened Negroes and we were going to raise our children with none of this race consciousness stuff. Well, that was just nonsense! We're not avoiding race anymore and I'm tired of trying to accommodate myself to these whites. Do you hear? I'm tired. Do you know what they did?" I was shouting uncontrollably now.

"Daddy, stop it. Please stop it. I don't want to hear this."

"Well, I'm going to tell you. They humiliated me in front of you. Can you understand that? Those bastards humiliated me in front of you! *Can you understand?* They think I'm an animal. I am not an animal. This is what they think of your father. That he is an animal! That he can be humiliated! That he can be..."

"Daddy!" Rosalind burst into the room. "Stop it! Leave her alone!"

"You!" I said savagely, "you! You, shut up! Just shut up!"

I turned back to Linnet.

"Do you understand this? Your father is nothing to them. *Nothing!* They hate black men. Everybody does. It's the national pastime. To hate black men. I am a black man. I am not an animal!"

"Daddy!" Linnet screamed. "Daddy, get out of here! Get out! Get out!"

Ida ran into the room. "Have you gone crazy, Gerald? Have you gone crazy? What are you doing to this child?"

I looked around, completely bewildered, at their astonished faces. They had never seen me act this way before. I had never said "shut up" to my children before. I felt cornered and frightened, and the people who stared at me at that moment were as much strangers to me as I was to them. I felt as if I were losing my mind completely; I could hardly believe how I was acting. Suddenly, my blood felt coldly dammed in my veins; I was struck dumb by the horror of what I had been doing. What had I wanted, coming into this room and badgering my daughter like this? What had I proved except that I wanted a certain kind of power over my children—not approval, but power? My outburst, partly a result of the enormous stress and public scrutiny I was experiencing, was not, finally, about racism, or my daughter's racial consciousness or lack thereof. It was perhaps about my own insecurities about race and maybe even about my insecurities as a parent, as a father. I might just as well have been trying to ravish that poor child, I thought later. At that moment, I felt as though I had. When we abuse our children it is often not from hate or dislike or even some rooted evil in us as adults, but rather some unintelligible outburst of ferocity, of longing. One is horrified by one's own loneliness, by one's child's loneliness, too.

"I—I—I," I started stammering, "I mean, I was just trying to explain…You don't understand…They think I'm an animal…I—oh, what the hell is the use?" I pushed past them and ran from the house.

It was a few days before Christmas, and the Frontenac incident, for better or for worse, was over. Ida and I made a conscious effort not to talk about it again after we received the "apology" from the mayor.

It was a cold day, but clear and bright. The sun was shining with a glassy brilliance. There were small mounds of dirty ice, trace memories of a small snowstorm. Linnet, wearing her "cool" jacket, and I, with my tweed cap, loafers, and blue wool jacket, walked along a street in Webster Groves. I told her a story.

"When I was in junior high school, well, it was a pretty bad school, largely black, with a lot of street gangs and that sort of thing. Well, one day, after school, which was when street gang wars most commonly erupted, this boy was killed, stabbed to death, right in front of the school. He was a white boy, a retarded boy. You see, they used to hold special-education classes for retarded kids in my junior high school. We hardly noticed these retarded kids because they were on a different schedule from the rest of the school, so they would usually be gone by the time we were dismissed.

"I don't know what happened that day or why the bus was late or how that kid got tangled up in our dismissal. But he was and a fight erupted and he was stabbed to death. Probably he was just in the way and no one had really intended to stab him at all.

"Well, the next day at school, the place is crawling with cops. They bust open all the lockers and search them for weapons. They walk up and down the hallway in a show of force.

"We had a special assembly that day and the vice principal, Mr. G., was reading us the riot act. I'm not paying that much attention, you know. I mean, I felt bad that that kid was killed, but I didn't do it and I couldn't have prevented it no matter how much I didn't want it to happen. Maybe the cops and all the white folks and everybody else was all upset because they couldn't have prevented it either and maybe they felt guilty and mad about that.

"Anyway, somewhere in this vice principal's harangue he said—and I'll never forget this— 'You act like animals, and we're going to treat you like animals.' I was just stunned. I couldn't believe what I heard. Well, the rest of the kids, you know, it was kind of like water rolling off a duck's back. They didn't care what the vice principal was talking about. But I never forgot that. And for the rest of the day I went around saying to myself, 'I'm not an animal.'"

"Did they catch the boys who killed the retarded boy?" Linnet asked.

"Yes, they caught them and put them away."

We were silent for a long time.

"It was bad," Linnet said finally, "to tell somebody that."

"Yes," I agreed, "it was too bad."

Linnet was quiet for a time. Then, suddenly, she blurted out, pleadingly:

"I'm sorry, Daddy. I'm sorry I wasn't with you

that night at the mall. If I was, then this wouldn't have happened. The guy wouldn't have called the police if I was walking with you."

It was a common practice for me to take my children with me whenever I went shopping, out for a walk in a white neighborhood, or just felt like going about in the white world. The reason was simple enough: if a black man is alone or with other black men, he is a threat to whites. But if he is with children, then he is harmless, adorable, the dutiful father. ("Only black men have to go around finding ways of defusing their presence in public all the time," one bitter black man said to me once and I sadly agreed.) After all, as Robert Frost suggested, no one takes his family with him on a robbery. Although I did this, I never thought that my children were ever aware of why I took them with me so much or that they would ever see the "political" signifi-cance of their presence. And especially I would never have thought Linnet would realize this as she seems so willfully oblivious to race and racial matters in this world. I was touched and humbled, moved not only by what she said, but by the depth of the realization it revealed.

"Thank you," I said, putting my arm on her shoulder, "thank you. It's nice to know I've got a daughter who can protect me."

THE MEANING OF BLOOD

To eat and to be eaten. The grain must be ground, the wine pressed; the bread must be broken. The true body is a body broken.

—Norman O. Brown, *Love's Body*

It was some several months after my oldest daughter, Linnet, had started menstruating that, on entering my daughters' bathroom one morning after they had departed for school, I found some sopping-wet, bloody panties in a corner behind the toilet. This was a decidedly curious but not necessarily disconcerting sight. I had grown up in a house with a widowed young mother and two older sisters, so discovering a piece of bloodstained women's underwear was scarcely a cause for alarm, although I must admit that during my years of growing up my mother and sisters made sure that my discovering any such things would be the sheerest of accidents. I was as protected from the secrets of femininity as it might be possible for a boy living with a group of women to be, although I heard, in the end, more than a bit about "female troubles." Until I was nine, my mother, my two sisters, and I slept in the same room. When I turned nine, we moved from an apartment to a small house; there, and for the remainder of my life there, I had a room of my own. As my mother put it, "A boy should have his own room," but it was just as likely that the women needed, as it were, to have a space to themselves. My sisters never did, which might explain why they were, on the whole, a bit more eager to go out on their own than I was.

I picked up the panties, a bit bemused about why they were so wet. Had she tried to wash them in the tub, or had she tried to flush them down the toilet? She had been having periods, by fits and starts, for some time now, so she could not have been frightened by the blood on that score anymore. She seemed, in fact, extraordinarily happy to finally begin her periods. Several of her friends of about the same age had already started months before her.

"So-and-so's period started today at school. Her mother had to pick her up early because so-and-so messed up her clothes," she would announce to me while eating her afternoon snack. It was almost as though in this world of adolescent girls the heavier the period the better. Usually the stories from school made me think that Linnet thought these girls were positively hemorrhaging into womanhood. On the whole, I was never quite sure how to respond to these stories. I had this picture in my mind that at the girl's bathroom in school, nonmenstruating girls would stand around beholding in awe the blood-smeared napkins of their menstruating sisters.

"Well, you are a perfectly healthy girl, so I am sure yours will start soon enough. You'll have to go through enough years of it, so I am sure there is no rush for this." The last I threw in as a kind of mimicry of her mother, who has complained bitterly about having periods since I have known her. "It's the only good thing about being pregnant," she said, "no periods." But it was being a bit of a wet blanket, at the very least, to tell a girl something like that, and it seemed, in retrospect, more than a little patronizing coming from a man. I wanted, in truth, very much to say, "Why don't you talk about this with your mother?" which she did, of course, but she seemed to have no real hesitation about discussing it with me. "Dear old Dad," we can tell him anything.

For seven years I washed my daughters regularly; first, every morning when they were babies, and then every night when they were toddlers and older. I had no especial relish for this task. It was simply something that had to be done and as my wife spent each evening washing dishes, I washed the children together in a little plastic tub, and then, when they outgrew this, in a standard bathtub. At first, I had to hold on to them, my forearms smeared with soap suds, for fear that they might slip and drown in seven inches of water.

"Does it hurt, you know, having a period?" she asked me once in the car.

"Well, not exactly, although one of my sisters, Rosalind, used to have terrible cramps and such. I guess it's called PMS today. She used to get terribly sick at times. I felt very sorry for her when I was a boy. But I don't think it really hurts very much. Your mother seems to get through the business in reasonably good shape."

I was a bit taken aback in her asking me instead of her mother, or as I found out later, in addition to her mother, who would be, in this instance, the undisputed expert. Yet she seemed to feel what I had to say about this to be as valuable as anything her mother might say. She seemed very much to want my opinion and my advice. Generally, this made me feel uneasy, bothered, burdened in a way that I did not wish to be. I was, after all, a man and, as I told Ida, I was not very interested in being feminized.

Perhaps because of the terribly misogynist stories I heard from boys and men during my childhood about the bodily functions of women, I was, in truth, slightly repelled by this blood business.

"Listen," I told Ida one evening, "I think it best if the girls keep all their women business to themselves or take it up with you. It's not my world and I don't feel comfortable dealing with it."

"What are we supposed to be?" Ida said in a huff. "Aliens? Creatures from Mars? What if I died? You would have to rear them and talk about 'their women business' unless you just gonna run out and get married again in a hurry. They don't tell you things they tell me, but they need two parents to talk to about their bodies. They need to talk to you about these things. If they didn't, they wouldn't come to you with it."

"I don't want to go to a children's doctor anymore," Rosalind announced to me in the car one day as we were going for her allergy shot.

"Why not?" I asked.

"Because I think I'm old enough to have the kind of doctor Mommy has," she said.

"I don't think so," I said. "Usually a woman

doesn't need a gynecologist until she starts having sex. You aren't even on your periods yet. You're a long way from needing that kind of doctor. It's no rush. You'll have one soon enough. What's the rush?"

She hung fire for a bit.

"Well, I just wanted a woman doctor," she said, at last.

"Gynecologists aren't women doctors. They're doctors who specialize in treating women. There are plenty of male gynecologists."

"Ugh," she spat out in disgust, "that's nasty. I would never go to a man for that. A man examining you with no clothes. That's awful. Who would go to a man doctor for that unless you're a man?"

"Say, Ida, I was wondering why you always go to male gynecologists. I thought, in this day and age, you would definitely go to a woman doctor."

"I did go to a woman gynecologist once. It made me feel funny. Getting an internal exam from a woman? I don't know. I didn't like it. There was something, I don't know, lesbian-like about it. I don't know. I just wasn't comfortable with a woman gynecologist and I sure don't want one."

❖

One Saturday morning recently, the girls and I watched *Just Another Girl on the IRT,* a film by a black woman director named Leslie Harris. It depicts the life of a bright, sassy black girl in a Brooklyn housing project who wants to be a doctor but who winds up pregnant. The film is rated R. Ida was more than a little dubious about this project.

"That film has a lot of cursing in it, all the typical black 'Hood street lingo," Ida objected. "Plus, I don't even see why you want them to watch it. It doesn't strike me as a particularly great movie."

"It's a film about a young black girl growing up," I responded. "That's a rare enough kind of film these days. I thought they might find that interesting. Besides, I'll watch it with them and explain stuff as it goes along."

Part of the reason I felt particularly insistent on watching this film with them was that a week before I had taken Rosalind to see the revival of the old Charlton Heston film *El Cid.* About ten or fifteen minutes into the film, Rosalind began squirming:

"I don't want to see this, Daddy. This is a boy's movie. I want to go home."

"No," I whispered in the darkness, "This is a classic movie. You'll enjoy it. Sit back and relax."

"I don't care if it's classic movie. It's just a boy's movie. It's boring. I don't want to watch this. I want to go home."

She was right. It was a boy's movie. A three-hour one at that.

So, I thought *Just Another Girl on the IRT,* a film that dealt with the female body from a female's perspective, would make up for this. A film about knowledge and the female body— about how women are, in some sense, like black people, denied knowledge of themselves and how this enforced ignorance can become self-destructive—seemed perfect for a session of "relating" to my girls.

We watched the film. Sometimes I would stop it to discuss a point. At other times either Rosalind or Linnet would ask me to stop it to ask something. They said very little while we watched.

"What did you think?" I asked when the movie ended.

"It was rotten," Linnet said. "The music was awful. The acting was awful. The story was awful."

"Yeah," said Rosalind, "it was the pits. The worst movie I ever saw. It was worse than *El Cid.*"

"You mean, you didn't find the story of this young black girl appealing?"

"Okay, Daddy," said Linnet, "if it'll make you feel any better, it was a great movie. You feel better?"

"No, I don't," I said, disappointed.

"Don't feel bad, Daddy. You tried. It was just a dumb movie, that's all."

"But why didn't you like it?"

"Well," said Linnet, "first, because it was about one of those Africa-crazy, Afrocentric kids. And I don't like those types of black kids and I don't think they're doing anything. But people make movies about them and every-thing just because they act mad. That seems to be a big thing for people, for blacks to act mad. The girl was just a loudmouth. The movie kept telling you she was supposed to be so smart, but all you ever see her doing is dumb things. Second, I thought the story was stupid. I'm not going to wind up getting pregnant by some dumb guy. I know about birth control and periods and all that stuff because we study it in school. I don't see why the movie couldn't end with her going to college, instead of being pregnant. Am I supposed to identify with that? Why should I? Just because I'm a black girl? Well, I don't. That movie may as well have been about a girl in Bosnia for all it meant to me. That wasn't my life on the screen. It was a dumb movie, Daddy. It's not your fault. You didn't make it."

"Yeah," Rosalind added, "it's not your fault, even though you did rent it and did have us waste two hours on a Saturday morning watching this junk that was worse than *El Cid* and *The Robe,* wasting a perfectly good Saturday morning when we could have been reading a book or been at the mall or something like that. Nope, absolutely not your fault!"

"Look, Gerald," Ida said later, "you learned a lesson with that film."

"What's that?" I asked, self-pityingly.

"Don't try to be relevant or politically correct in order to relate to your kids. I'm surprised you made a mistake like that, since you hate relevancy and political correctness as modes of dealing with people. I told you to listen to them when they wanted to be listened to about their bodies. I didn't tell you to start trying to force the issue. So you made a mistake. Forget about it. You learned something valuable about your kids and maybe about yourself as well."

"So be it," I said, smiling at her.

Halloween (from Rosalind Early's diary, verbatim)

November 1, 1992

Yesterday was Halloween. It was fun I invited a friend from my old school to trick or treat with me. It was Sarah W. who is Jewish and was my best friend before we moved. She was dressed as Death but wouldn't hold the reaper thing that Death holds because her father made it and didn't want to mess it up. I was dressed as an Angel. Some pair we were, huh? We walked until it began to rain then after the rain stopped we walked until my mom said we had to go inside. My dad asked me why I like Sarah and I said that in school we could talk and the same kids didn't like us so we became friends.

Many things have happened over the month of October, like my dad going to the hospital. Making a few new friends and getting my first scoop of skittles. It's been a very jam packed month one that I learned a lot and thought about others one month I'd like to keep, put away and cherish forever.

BIRTH AND TRUST

Nothing can be sole or whole
That has not been rent.

> —W. B. Yeats, *"Crazy Jane Talks*
> *with the Bishop"*

When Rosalind was born, on a warm Thanksgiving Day in 1981 at Tompkins County Hospital, Ithaca, New York, I thought I would feel at least vaguely disappointed because she was not a boy. Ida thought I very much wanted a boy, and I suppose we tossed around boys' names more than girls'.

"You men always want sons," she said during the pregnancy.

"I am not so sure I do," I replied. "I don't know what to teach a boy. I had no father to teach me."

As soon as the doctor held her up, I could plainly see that I was fated to be the father of another girl. All I could think of at that moment was: "Good, it's a girl. No separate bedrooms."

As I remember, I was not very thrilled about having a second child, at least, not at the time. I was trying to finish up graduate school and Ida was working as a secretary. We had no money and life was difficult. Sometimes we were so broke that I had to wash baby clothes in a tub with a washboard and Octagon soap just as I had seen my mother do with my sisters' clothes when I was a child. The smell of Octagon soap would permeate the whole house, and for the entire day my mother's fore-arms and the air of the apartment smelled like freshly cleaned laundry. I liked the smell so much that I wanted my mother to wash me in Octagon soap.

"Don't be silly," she told me. "That soap's for washing clothes."

"You were a silly boy," Rosalind said, when I told her the story, "wanting to get washed with laundry soap!"

By doing some of our laundry in a tub, we saved a few precious dollars. I stayed at home every day working on my dissertation while Ida worked. I would go to the library at night. The only time we could hire a baby-sitter was three times a week for about two hours while I taught my class. At one point, when Ida could no longer work, we went on welfare. It was the most humiliating moment of my life then: in the dirty, stinking office with all those dirty, stinking down-and-out people, the heartless, thoroughly bored caseworkers asking a bunch of prying, depersonalizing questions in some display of petty bureaucratic power. ("This is the way the world ends, This is the way the world ends," I sang to Ida as we waited our turn, "Not with a bang but with a bureaucrat.") Everything in the office—the procedure, the attitude of the caseworker, the walls, the floor, the desks, the chairs—all meant to remind us, the dirty and the stinking and the down-and-out, that we were nothing, less than nothing. It was as if, in one fantastically bleak setting, it were possible to be held in contempt, considered with indifference, and condescended to in pity. And there we both sat, I in my dirty down coat, Ida in her cheap "Republican" cloth coat with slightly run-over shoes, and Linnet, sealed in the snowsuit that Ida's parents had given us. When we left the office, we sat in our parked car a long time. Ida, dumpy in her pregnancy, holding Linnet, was depressed and felt completely degraded. My anger was nearly volcanic:

"Never," I said, turning to Ida, trying to control my voice, "never, if I have to work a thousand jobs a day, will I set foot in a welfare office again. I'd rather clean toilets for a dollar an hour than take anything from the government because I'm poor. In fact, I think stealing is more honorable than this."

These were the hard, stressful, "young married" years. When Ida first told me she was pregnant with Rosalind, about eighteen months after the birth of Linnet, I was unhappy. Indeed, I stayed unhappy during the whole pregnancy.

"I think it's crazy for us to have another child right now," I said to Ida. "We don't have any money. I'm trying to finish this dissertation. We ought to wait until I'm finished school. When I get a job, things will be better."

"So, what do you want me to do? Have an abortion?" she asked.

"Well, that's up to you. But it might not be a bad idea."

"It's a very bad idea," she responded coolly. "Having children is always inconvenient. When your mother had you and your father died just nine months later and she was left alone, a black woman with no education and no money, with three children, the oldest being five, I'll bet she thought you were real inconvenient. But she didn't treat you that way. This child is going to be good for us, just wait and see."

As the months went by and Ida did not terminate the pregnancy, I became resigned to another child and hoped, in a way, for a girl, simply because it would be cheaper since we already had one. But I was grouchy and self-pitying throughout the pregnancy, and whenever the subject came up in the early days I was likely to badger Ida:

"Isn't my life hard enough out here without having a herd of babies? Is it asking too much just to postpone for a year or two having the second one? Is that asking too much?"

"Yes," Ida responded, "it is asking too much. I want to have it now."

"As a black woman, what kind of help are you to me? All you're doing is bringing me down by having babies when we're not ready for them. Life is tough enough dealing with the white world as it is. But how are you helping?"

"What is this? Your Walter Lee Younger, *Raisin in the Sun* speech? 'I'm just a poor, put-upon black man and the whole world is in a conspiracy against me!' Don't give me that crap! What's race got to do with any of this?" Ida said with a sharp laugh. "Unless you think that if you had a white wife she'd be more disposed to having babies on the schedule you have in mind. She just might be. But I'm having this one now. This child is not going to make life any tougher than it already is."

Rosalind began her inconvenience on the day she was born. Ida and I had planned a nice

Thanksgiving dinner with the trimmings (we had saved up for this), a real family affair as Linnet was now old enough, at two, to enjoy the fare with us. Unfortunately, Ida's labor started at six o'clock Thanksgiving morning, and Rosalind was born around one in the afternoon. Nothing had been cooked. I picked up Linnet from a friend who had graciously kept her while Ida gave birth. At home, I tried to make stuffing, clean vegetables, bake a pie, and cook a twenty-pound turkey all in three hours. This dinner was a disaster. I ate half-raw, half-burnt turkey breast and Linnet ate a hot dog as we listened to some McCoy Tyner and Sonny Fortune records.

On Rosalind's first day home, she cried—yelled, really—the whole night. Linnet slept through it all, but neither Ida nor I caught a wink of sleep that night. Finally, around six or so she went off into a deep sleep for several hours, while Ida and I watched the sun rise.

"I guess she's going to be one of those kids who really speaks her likes and dislikes," Ida said.

I was furious for a moment, but then we both looked at each other and started to laugh. "I guess she will at that."

And know this about Rosalind Early: when she is angry she becomes, unlike most people, amazingly articulate. Her parents and sister learned this at their peril.

From time to time, either Linnet or Rosalind will wish aloud for a baby brother.

"Don't you wish you had a son, Daddy?" I am asked frequently by Linnet, who thinks we ought to adopt a child. "A baby somewhere needs us" is how she puts it.

I have considered the possibility of adopting. Not so much because I desire a son; in many ways I was relieved at having daughters. They seemed easier to rear and I felt, frankly, more comfortable in a house of women than in a house of men. I have never fully known how I am to act around men, what sort of things I'm supposed to say, how I am to carry myself. Whenever I am in the company of men I am not truly myself but always someone who is looking at himself trying to act as a man should when he is with other men. (I have always looked up to men, though, admired them as I have never admired any woman.) But this should not be taken as a preference for the world of women: having been around women all my life, I was usually happy to be away from them for extended periods of time. I have always seen the ideal world as one of enduring, stoic men; but I have always understood the *real* world as a place of women.

Adopting a child is something that has been pressed upon me by a certain guilt. After all, I am middle-class black man and there are plenty of black children who need to be adopted.

"What's the matter, Daddy?" Linnet chimed once. "You think to yourself, 'I'm busy and now is not the right time.' Heck, it's never the right time to have children. Do you know that we guys are always inconvenient?"

Once, when having this conversation about adopting, Linnet, Rosalind, and I wound our way around to the subject of abortion.

"We're sitting here talking about having another child. But we haven't asked your mother. We don't know if she would want to adopt a child. Maybe she doesn't want any more children. You know, if she were, by some incredible chance, to get pregnant again, she might have an abortion or something." I said this half kiddingly, and, in retrospect, I wish I hadn't. I knew that if Ida were to become pregnant again, there would be virtually no consideration of an abortion. Linnet simply nodded and grinned.

"Yeah," she said, "Mommy's a career woman now."

But Rosalind became so visibly upset that when I noticed her stricken face I was stunned.

"What do you mean, have an abortion?" Rosalind yelled. "What's being a career woman got to do with having a baby? What's having a job got to do with having a baby? Mommy wouldn't have an abortion, would she, Daddy? You guys wouldn't have an abortion, would you?"

I stared at her, slack jawed, surprised, and more than a little unnerved by her vehemence. "Well, no. I was just kidding around. If your mother was pregnant, we would not have an abortion."

Somehow, this outburst should not have surprised me as much as it did. I simply hadn't thought Rosalind's views through to their ultimate logical conclusions on any variety of matters on which she was likely to have an opinion. Rosalind tends to respond very strongly to certain issues that, I suppose, are a matter of justice with her. Two, in particular, are her own personal rights (a point of great interest to her as a second child who always seems to have followed in her sister's wake), and the right for children not to be harmed, for she thinks the world is largely a place that wishes to hurt children because they are helpless.

For instance, on the first point, both my daughters had security blankets for several years. Linnet dragged around an infant's blanket until she was seven, when Ida decided to take it, frayed and worn, from her. For the first few years of Linnet's "addiction," we were both sympathetic because Linnet seemed under so much stress and the blanket, when she came home from the baby-sitter's or from school, was such an obvious source of comfort. The expression on her face when she would pick it up and stroke it was much like a cat's on catnip, or someone completely relaxed not by a drug but by an ambience. She looked as if she were in a beatific state of stupor.

"That child comes in here and zones out on that blanket, as if it were a narcotic or something," Ida said one day, vehemently. "We need to get rid of it. It's making her immature and incapable of coping with her problems."

So, afraid that she might not take this denial well at all and that we might have to abandon this course of action after a few days and give the blanket back, Ida merely hid the blanket in a closet but told Linnet that it had accidentally been thrown out. Surprisingly, after a few days of looking around for it, and missing it a great deal, she adjusted and soon forgot about it. When this happened Ida began warning Rosalind about her blanket fetish too.

"When you're seven, you're going to have give up your blanket too, just like Linnet did," Ida would remind Rosalind from time to time.

I found it easier to justify taking Rosalind's blanket away, largely because I never took her attachment to it very seriously. I thought she had simply imitated Linnet and adopted the habit to be like her sister and eventually found herself hooked. But when the time came, it turned out to be a lot harder than "with-drawal" was for Linnet. When Rosalind turned seven, I hid her blanket as well. After a few days, she demanded its return:

"I want my blanket back," she told me.

"It's not here," I lied. "Your mother and I told you it's gone."

"I think you hid it in the house. I want my blanket back," she insisted.

"Even if we did," I equivocated, "you can't have it back. We told you that at the age of seven we were going to take your blanket. We did it with Linnet. That's the rule in this household. No security blankets after the age of seven."

"I don't care. I want my blanket back," she countered. "Why do I have to do something because Linnet does it? You guys always do that. I have to do it because Linnet does it. That's not right. I'm not Linnet. I want to be treated like Rosalind, not Linnet. I want my blanket back. It's mine. It's not yours."

"Listen, Rosalind," I said, trying to be a bit more stern, "as your parent, I have the right to take things from you when I don't think you should have them anymore. Your mom and I thought you shouldn't have the blanket anymore."

"But you didn't tell me why. The blanket wasn't hurting me. It's mine. You should respect my things. You don't have a right to take my things when they don't hurt me."

"Rosalind," I said, exasperated, "the blanket is gone and you're not getting it back. I'm not going to debate it." Frankly, I felt ridiculous arguing with a seven-year-old girl about my actions in her behalf. Partly I felt ridiculous and uncomfortable because she seemed to have the upper hand in the exchange.

On the second point—the right of children not to be harmed—Rosalind has had many outbursts or moments of concern, especially whenever she reads the papers, discovering another child murder or child molestation case. Recently, for instance, there have been several child murders in St. Louis, girl children taken by some mysterious man as they walked home from school. Rosalind began to have occasional nightmares about her own abduction.

"Look, Rosalind," I said, after she told me about her latest nightmare, "why don't you carry a little can of red pepper in your book bag? Then, if any strange man accosts you while you are walking home from school, just throw the stuff in his face and run. Believe me, red pepper will disable that sucker." I thought the suggestion to be sound: red pepper was perfectly legal, not dangerous to herself or to someone else should she throw or spill it by mistake, and it would give her some sense of protection as well. But Rosalind saw the matter differently.

"What kind of a dumb suggestion is that?" she demanded. "I don't want any red pepper. That's only going to make me feel more nervous, going to school with that. That's only going to have me think about it more. Your ideas are dumb, Daddy. Leave me alone."

That Rosalind would have a strong feeling about abortion, and that she would have the kind of view she did, should not, therefore, have jolted me as much as it did. And it was ultimately not the view that bothered me as much as the vehemence with which it was stated. Here was something that she had thought about on her own very carefully for some time and that I knew nothing about until that moment. I suppose it was the unexpectedness of this view as well that dismayed me, the fact that I had never even mentioned abortion to my children before, so I hardly thought they had any views, one way or another, on the subject.

"What are you getting so excited about, Ros?" Linnet said casually. "Lots of women get abortions. Sometimes it's necessary."

"No," Rosalind screamed, "it's never necessary. How could any parent think about getting an abortion? If you don't want babies, then don't have sex. If you and mommy had aborted me, I wouldn't be here. Everybody talks about a fetus like it's a thing. But everybody starts out that way. If I had been killed as a fetus, I would be dead. I wouldn't be here. How could anybody do that to a child? We trust you. It's wrong! It's wrong! Abortion is wrong!" Tears were rolling down her cheeks. She was nearly hysterical.

"When you get older," I said, trying to be soothing, "you might look at it differently. You might think that there would be a time when an abortion might be a correct procedure. Women are raped, beaten, abused. Besides, women ought to have some control over when

they have children. I think you may be person-
alizing this thing..."

But Rosalind assured me and Linnet that she
would never change as she grew older. She kept
talking about trust and that adults wanted to
destroy children because it was convenient. Of
course it was personal. The whole world is personal, after all. And she wasn't interested in
women's rights, just her right to stay alive and
not have adults harm children. "Why should I
have to die because it's not a perfect world for
women? It's wrong," she said, running from
the room. "And nothing you or Linnet will tell
me will make me think it's right."

Linnet and I were silent.

"That girl's always flying off the deep end,"
Linnet said at last.

"Maybe, in this case, she had reason to," I
said quietly.

"If you ask me, it's just another case of her
getting worked up over nothing," Linnet said,
strolling from the room.

No, I thought, she was worked up, indeed,
over quite a something, and rightly so. I waited
a bit and then went up to her room. I knocked
and she bade me enter. She was playing on the
floor with one of her dolls. I sat on the edge of
the bed. She did not look up at me. What she

had said earlier made me feel more uncomfortable than it should have. It made me feel guilty
because I had once thought of aborting her out
of convenience. But that was different, I
thought. I was just a poor student. Besides, she
had not been a real person in any sense. It was
not the same as if I wanted to get rid of her
now. Or perhaps it was. Her passionate outburst had skewered me with doubt. Perhaps it
was a violation of some implicit and invisible
trust in the world between parents and children, a trust that forms a kind of background
music, a rhythm, for their dance together. I
decided to change the subject entirely. She's
such a lovable kid, I thought, sitting there. And
somehow, at that moment, I wanted her
approval again, her trust.

"You know," I began, "when you were a
kid, you didn't like me at all. You preferred
your mother and I could never do anything to
please you. I was kind of jealous about this.
Besides, I had spent so much time with Linnet
that she preferred me to your mother. So I
thought I had a bit of a touch with the ladies,
you might say. But it took a long time before
you felt comfortable with me, until you were
four or five. I was very hurt by the rejection."

"Well, come on, Daddy. I was just a dumb

old baby then. I like you just fine now. In fact, you're one of my favorite people. How I felt about you when I was a year old is nothing to get down in the mouth about."

A time comes when a parent confronts a child with a certain weight of guilt, oppressed by its burden, yet blessed by its immovable inevitability to produce, with its prayers and curses, through a brief shifting, a kind of spiral of mercy. Oddly enough, I thought this a very generous thing for her to say. I felt relieved and even, in some ways, forgiven.

"In our house," I said, rising from the bed, "we respect each other's opinion. I respect yours and I have always said that you were entitled to it. And it might do us well to consider the weight of our opinions as we consider the weight of our responsibilities. You have taught me that today. An opinion is not something just to go mouthing off. It is a responsibility to have it, hold it, bear it, believe in it."

She looked at me, puzzled but pleased that at least there would be no more argument on this day.

"What's your opinion on abortion, Daddy? I mean, what do you really think? Do you think I'm right?" she asked, becoming again a child.

That, I felt, was an absolutely dangerous

question, under these circumstances. I might have been a stumbling dancer in some of this parenthood business, but I wasn't about to lose my stride with that jangling discord. A parent's opinion cannot always be the prize for a child's sense of worth.

"You know," I said, laughing, as I left the room, "the greatest favor a father can do for a daughter is to never agree with her opinions."

A POEM FOR ROSALIND

A few days after Ros's outburst on abortion, I wrote a poem for her. I had been trying, for the longest time, to write one for her, in part because I felt she might be jealous of the fact that I had written a few for Linnet (although she never mentioned it), and in part because I wanted to show both her and myself that I had some sense of who she was—enough, at least, to be able to capture in a poem. Somehow, what she said about abortion finally fixed a certain notion in my head, made me see something. The poem came relatively easy after that. She read it without much expression—indeed, seemed singularly unimpressed by it. "It's okay," she said quietly, tossing it aside. I was a bit hurt by that, but perhaps it was not much of a poem anyway. Later in the day, though, she ran up to Linnet saying, "Read this poem Daddy wrote for me." For several weeks the poem was posted on her bedroom door.

Why isn't Marseilles said the way it looks?
(FOR MY YOUNGEST DAUGHTER, ROSALIND)

Sitting in the center, more or less, of
Her room, surrounded on either side of
Her by dolls, black and white, plastic and
Cloth, naked and clothed; by books, some
Picture, some all prose, a very used copy
Of Trumpet of the Swan tented out on its edge
So precariously as if it dare not collapse;
By dirty sneakers, scuffed "Sunday" shoes, and
Six different "hand-me-down" dresses from
Her big sister's closet that, as she says,
"Ought to go back to big sister or to the poor
Because little sister does not like them";
By pages of piano music that refuse to be practiced;
By a half-scribbled notebook with copy from
The encyclopedia for tomorrow's book report;

She eyes herself in a hand-held mirror, smiling
Just so smiling as if pleased as punch by some
Prettier-than-thou image of a little girl swinging

Her just-pressed hair to-and-fro as if this small
    gesture
Pantomimes an answer to the question of why
Things are the way they sound instead of how they
    look;
This waif, kiddingly cunning, who, in her eye's corner,
When seeing someone watching, is inclined by a
Generosity that not even she suspects she has
To grant forgiveness as a small careless gift pulled
From the largess of her abundant stocks of glory.

"...TO KNOW YOU'RE ALIVE"

*For I have the blessing of God in the three Points
of manhood, of the pen, of the sword, & of chivalry.*

    —Christopher Smart, *Rejoice in
    the Lamb*

Stretched out against a blue, hard, indifferent sky,
Taut and poised as a dancer's muscled stillness,
As a mouse upon a cat's bare, bloody throat,
As the bloody lines of empire dimly netting the
    throes,
As the distant church-spire pressed tight against
    the wire,
Is the season of our joy and pain flung in its
    dimensions

*Of balls and strikes and fouls and errors and outs
    and pauses,*
*Boredom and spit, a soft, soft waster of time, the
    irrelevant*
*Gallantry of outfielders outstretched for catches:
    The Game.*
*And this we watch—o splendid errand—against
    the blue, hard sky,*
The men below in a child's game that only, then,
Those men, magically, can play to provide, in grace,
*For us, the throng, at last, the will to outlast that
    sorrow*
*Against which this dubious contentment is our
    only flight*
*To a tremulous childhood of tumultuous peace,
    that, spoken in the*
*Tragic speech of prayer, alas, can bring us, rejoicing
    in that*
*Regeneration abounding (This, then, the only love
    that's left*
*In that stolen expanse of our glory!), fairly struck
    in the sunlit*
Reaches of our grievance and our divine repair.

> —Gerald Early, "The Green Fields of
> America (Paths of Our Republic)"

There is a certain sweet but taut madness that
descends upon the culture during the late sum-

mer and early fall. Those who are lovers of baseball know this as the "pennant chase." In the dead of summer, the long season moves along with a bit of contented leisure, with the assurance that, after all, for everyone, players and fans alike, there is always another game. But suddenly with the advent of autumn, there is the ferocious realization that not only will it end but it must end—what might be called, to borrow a term from a famous musician, a ferocious longing to come to its own resolution at last. And it is during these days, when light is less, that watching a baseball game is a bit like taking the final measurement of an unavoidable metaphysical truism: namely, that enacted on the field is the proposition that the urgency of an implacable fate always thwarts the expectancy of a well-tempered design. In other words, nature is not bound to obey any plan, no matter how wonderfully constructed. It is the old saw about man proposing but God disposing. It is a rule that I learned from being a passionate lover of baseball since I was a boy.

If I could have run around as a boy with a tin whistle, a water pistol, a foldable kite, a large collection of bats and sticks and gloves for baseball and stickball, and my newspapers and shopping bags, I would have been ecstatically happy and I could have died at the age of twelve and never felt I missed anything in life—not sex, not education, not adulthood, not marriage, not family.

"My sister Rosalind first taught me about the game of baseball—not playing it, but following the pro game," I told Linnet and Rosalind. "She taught me about a team called the Milwaukee Braves and about players named Hank Aaron, Eddie Matthews, and Joe Adcock. I must have been about six or seven, because it was the late fifties, when the Braves were a championship team. I have always had an interest in them ever since because of that. She also gave me baseball cards and taught me how to read a box score."

"You learned about baseball from a girl?!" Rosalind said, "From my Aunt Rosalind? That's something."

The single desire that dominated my search for delight was simply to love and to be loved.

—Saint Augustine, *The Confessions*

There was a week where I took first Rosalind, then Linnet, to baseball games with me. I have had season's tickets to the St. Louis Cardinals now for a few years, but my daughters do not go to the games with me very often. I dreamed of teaching them how to score the games and making them fans, but at the games themselves they take very little interest in them. I showed them how to score: Rosalind picked it up fairly easily but was soon very bored with it. Linnet never truly understood it and I did not press the matter as, after all, there was no need, in my mind, to make attending a baseball game something like going to school all over again. What always interested them about going to the games, aside from the food (children, I suppose, will always be thrilled at the chance of eating bad, cheap, greasy food somewhere outside home), was my own love of the game. I could sometimes feel them looking at me, hunched in my seat, watching the game with a kind of tension that would not indicate love at all but agony and anxiety. I never cheer plays, never boo failure; indeed, except at moments when I provide them with some commentary on what is going on, I am usually silent.

One afternoon during a particular week when we had seen games nearly back-to-back, they were looking at a picture of me when I was boy of about eight. It is the only picture they have seen of me as a boy (so few were taken, and most of those were lost). I am standing, with three other boys, in front of the altar of my church. We are all in our Sunday best, but I am the only one wearing a coat—a trench coat, buttoned to my throat. I remember the coat well and the day of the picture. It was an Easter Sunday. I am smiling to beat the band in the picture.

"You were a cute little boy," Linnet said, holding the picture out to me.

"Yeah," said Rosalind, laughing, "big happy smile, big block head."

"I wish I could have known you when you were a boy," Linnet said, almost with a tone of poignant regret.

"Me, too," said Rosalind. "I bet you were a nice little boy."

"You guys don't even like boys," I said grinning. "Besides, you wouldn't have liked me. I was a boring little boy. All I liked was baseball. It was all I thought about as a boy. It was all I wanted to play. I loved to play it and I loved to watch the professionals play it."

"Why did you like baseball so much, Daddy?" Linnet asked.

"You know," I said, casting my mind back a bit, "there would be these days, terribly hot summer days, and no one when I was a boy had air-conditioning except the movie houses, a few corner grocery stores, and a couple of the Italian homeowners in the neighborhood. Well, on those days especially, there would be a group of us black boys who would get together to play baseball, softball, stickball, anything, somewhere in the heat. All day long that is what we would do. And before each game, just as we saw done in the major-league games, we would sing the national anthem, the whole bunch of us, before we played a game. Can you imagine that? A group of black boys out in some lot in the heat singing the national anthem? We didn't even like the song and most of us didn't like to sing but we did because that was how the professionals did it. Well, it was at those moments of singing the national anthem like that, a bunch of raggedy black boys, that I really loved baseball most of all because it made me feel like an American. I felt like I was part of the country."

They were silent for a time, I suppose more impressed by this response than they should have been.

"But," I said suddenly, "that's not all. That's not quite it. I mean, I loved baseball, watching the pros play because I was a fatherless boy without brothers and so I could watch those young men and imagine one of them as an older brother or as my father. I loved baseball as a boy because..."

As I was saying this my thoughts drifted back to my father and how much I, when I was a boy, wished I could have known him, not as a man, but when he was a boy. I wished that I could have grown up with him, that he could have been my best friend, that we could have sung the national anthem together, and could have gone to games. My father and I would walk arm in arm, a fantasy so intense that I would sometimes see him before me, imagine him there, talk to him. So intense a fantasy was it that at times as a child I thought my make-believe was a sure sign that I was crazy. Whose little boy are you? For years, I lied to my childhood friends, telling them that my father wanted to name me after him, wanted to name me Henry.

"He wanted to," I would say proudly, "but my mom wouldn't let him." But I knew, all along, the story that he hated his name, that he would never have given it to me. But all children wish to know their parents as children, wish to know the origin of these people who rather spring upon them fully grown, fully developed, fully being what they are.

I finished my thought to my daughters: "...because it made me feel less lonely."

"Well," said Linnet, after a moment, "we still wish we could have known you as a boy. You were probably real nice. Not like the boys we know. I bet it would have been fun going to a baseball game with you when you were a boy."

"Yea," said Rosalind, "going to a baseball game with that smiley little boy with the big block head. That would have been fun."

I remembered what I had once read in the Richard Wright novel *The Outsider,* about the tragic protagonist, Cross Damon: "It was the restrictions of marriage, the duties to children, obligations to friends, to sweethearts, and blood kin that he had struck at so blindly and—gallantly?" But it was in the very "restrictions of marriage" and of family life that I had gained the greatest sense of freedom and the highest form of liberation. For it was through being bound to others that I found that I could lose myself, escape the entrapment of solipsism, cease the restless search for that fulfillment of myself simply through acts of absorption.

During a tense moment in our marriage, many years ago, Ida and I sat across from one another, I on a crate and she on a piano bench. It was a Sunday afternoon. We had just come from church, and it was then that I had to decide if I wanted to stay married.

"Do you want a life," she asked me, "or just the trappings of a life? Do you want to grow or do you simply wish to say, 'I had these things, some experiences with women.' You're not wrong if you want something else, Gerald. But dammit, you've got to want what you want."

"I want my children," I said, quietly, and after a moment, "to understand the qualities of devotion and virtue."

"Well, you can live it, hope for the best, and

be called a fool. Or not live it, hope for the best, and be called a hypocrite," Ida said.

Later that same afternoon, while Ida sat at the kitchen table flipping through catalogues and I rummaged through the pots and pans to begin making Sunday dinner, I felt for a moment—considering the scene—how much life goes on, that a certain kind of serenity, ironically, transcends even the greatest domestic turbulence. I turned to Ida, measuring my words with some care:

"I'm ashamed to admit it but I have not always *tried* to be a good man. There were times when it was easier not to be and I took the easy way. And although I tried much harder, I have sometimes failed as a husband and I'm sure you've been disappointed in me from time to time. But I have never *not* tried to be a good father. Never! I may not always have succeeded, but I've never stopped *trying* to be a good father. I can bear the price I must pay for my lack of vigilance in some aspects of my life, but never for any lack of vigilance as a father."

And Ida, legs crossed, tilted her head as the late afternoon sun came through the kitchen window, tinting her hair, splashing on the table like a light water, and, without looking directly at me, smiled. It was the first time in a while that she had done that and I smiled too.

"Try?" she said softly. "Try? *Anybody* can try. Trying is nothing. Succeeding is everything in this world and in this life."

I cocked my head a bit, recognizing my own rhetoric—exactly the same words I would say to myself when I had not done well on some writing project or in the classroom, exactly the same words I would say to Linnet or Rosalind to goad them to achieve. I had been told as a boy that Babe Ruth had once said those same words to Joe Louis shortly before Louis fought for the title. It had always stayed with me.

Her smile had broadened to a grin. She was simply badgering me in a playful way with my own bromides. She looked almost happy, and very girlish, like someone, some pink-dressed girl, a boy would ask to dance.

"Some people have succeeded more than they think they have," she said. "Besides, don't put too much pressure on yourself to be more than anybody's got a right to expect. I wouldn't be much of a woman if I couldn't deal with some disappointments and you wouldn't be much of a man if you couldn't deal with them either.

"You know," she continued, out of the blue, "I could never play Pinochle. Could never learn to play the game. At least, not with you Philadelphia Negroes. The cards moved too fast and I was always getting my head rubbed."

"I guess I'm not a typical Philadelphia Negro. I could never play it either. The same thing happened to me," I said musingly.

"Well, what's for dinner?" she asked.

Shortly after this conversation with Ida, I thought of my mother, who during all of her years of widowhood, all my growing-up years, adolescent years, young-adult years, had never had a man spend the night in our house. I had been permitted to grow up free from the emotional entanglements of her life, never burdened with how my mother felt about some man, or if she suffered. I had been free to think only and constantly about myself. Such a wonderful gift to give to a child! When I became an adult I thought this such a sacrifice.

"Listen," my mother said to me once recently, "why make your life harder than you have to? I sacrificed, but I never denied myself anything." What I learned in this conversation with my mother was that you do what you have to, not so that you can do what you want but because doing what you have to is what you want. There was no trace of sentimentality when she said this, and I realized there was none because, after all, she had done this as much for herself as for her children, because she had never, once, felt an ounce of sentimentality about having children or living with them.

And so I thought as well, then, at that moment, thinking about my mother, Why make my life harder than I have to?

I looked at my daughters, and my boyhood picture, and appreciated the gift of parenthood, at that moment, more than any other gift I have ever been given. For what person, except one's own children, would want so deeply and sincerely to have shared your childhood? Who else would think your insignificant and petty life so precious in the living, so rich in its expressiveness, that it would be worth partaking of what you were to understand what you are? And so in the end I fulfill my needs by discovering that I mean this much to my children, more than I could possibly mean to anyone else. Sidney Poitier once wrote, "The word 'Daddy' held some magical connotations for me." But it was the absence of the word in my own life, never having called anyone that, that made me think it less a naming of a category than the unstoppable expression of an artifice that imagines itself an aspiration. That someone would call me what I had always yearned to call someone else was not a fulfillment but a triumphant disquietude, a quirky, spotty redemption.

I could not stop laughing at the sheer wonder of the thought. So I laughed and laughed, though my daughters, nonplussed, did not, I am sure, think that the picture of the big-headed boy smiling to beat the band was as funny as all that.

Mr. Rogers is right: it *is* such a good feeling to know you're alive.